Off Grid Living

A Starter Guide For Anyone Thinking About A Self-sufficient Living

(Step-by-step Guide From Planning To Building A Homestead To Living)

Paul Rios

Published By **Ryan Princeton**

Paul Rios

All Rights Reserved

Off Grid Living: A Starter Guide For Anyone Thinking About A Self-sufficient Living (Step-by-step Guide From Planning To Building A Homestead To Living)

ISBN 978-1-77485-680-2

No part of this guidebook shall be reproduced in any form without permission in writing from the publisher except in the case of brief quotations embodied in critical articles or reviews.

Legal & Disclaimer

The information contained in this ebook is not designed to replace or take the place of any form of medicine or professional medical advice. The information in this ebook has been provided for educational & entertainment purposes only.

The information contained in this book has been compiled from sources deemed reliable, and it is accurate to the best of the Author's knowledge; however, the Author cannot guarantee its accuracy and validity and cannot be held liable for any errors or omissions. Changes are periodically made to this book. You must consult your doctor or get professional medical advice before using any of the suggested remedies, techniques, or information in this book.

Upon using the information contained in this book, you agree to hold harmless the Author from and against any damages, costs, and expenses, including any legal fees potentially resulting from the application of any of the information provided by this guide. This disclaimer applies to any damages or injury caused by the use and application, whether directly or indirectly, of any advice or information presented, whether for breach of contract, tort, negligence, personal injury, criminal intent, or under any other cause of action.

You agree to accept all risks of using the information presented inside this book. You need to consult a professional medical practitioner in order to ensure you are both able and healthy enough to participate in this program.

TABLE OF CONTENTS

Introduction 1

Chapter 1: What Exactly Does Mean To Be "Off From The Grid"? 2

Chapter 2: Alternative Energy Off The Grid 51

Chapter 3: Composting In An Off Grid Environment 66

Chapter 4: Living Off-Grid In A Motorhome 78

Chapter 5: Methods Of Preserving Food 104

Chapter 6 Security And Protection Off-Grid 116

Chapter 7"The "Business In Front" Strategy 131

Chapter 8: Benefits Of Living Off The Grid Living 148

Chapter 9: Provocative Challenges For Off The Grid 154

Chapter 10: What Do You Need For Off The Grid Living? 160

Chapter 11: The Way Minimalism Will Help Your Transition Towards Off The Grid Living 167

Conclusion 184

Introduction

Are you a fan of the idea of living completely off the grid appealing? It's not just you who thinks like this. A lot of Americans are opting to break away from the demands and utility lines of common areas and go on their own, which is leading in the rise of an off-grid lifestyle.

It's important to keep in mind that living off the grid isn't just about rustic individualism or a cottage-style. There's plenty that goes when you live off grid, and there's a lot to think about before you decide if it's the right choice and includes some important financial aspects to consider. This article will provide a brief overview of what living off the grid entails and also the answers to some frequently requested questions about this peculiar method of living.

Chapter 1: What Exactly Does Mean To Be "Off From The Grid"?

Living off grid means staying away from standard infrastructures for utilities, including municipal water, power gas, sewer infrastructures.

Off-grid homes are self-sufficient by utilizing their own systems to provide vital services such as the solar energy and private wells. People who live off the grid often do not have the internet, particularly when it comes to services like internet at home and phone lines.

It is true that there are pros and cons with this lifestyle. Regarding advantages, living off of the grid can help people live more sustainably and effectively. It also allows you to cut down on the cost of energy costs (though as we'll learn in the following section living off grid isn't cheap initially).

What are the disadvantages of living off the grid? First of all you'll need to leave behind a number of modern facilities, including air conditioners and washing machines along with microwaves and Wi-Fi, in order in order to survive completely by yourself. Additionally, you'll be unable to access the assistance which is provided by being connected to utility grids of municipal utilities. There isn't a municipal agency that is automatically assigned to repair your solar or well when it fails. The homeowner is responsible for most, if not all of the expenses and obligations of managing your home that isn't an easy task even for the most committed people who live off grid.

How much will living off the grid really cost you?

Living off the grid will let you free yourself from monthly energy cost. But there are a lot of costs upfront to think about and it's not as easy or as affordable as buying a piece of land and starting the business.

Here are a few expenses to be considered when deciding whether an off-grid lifestyle is possible for you:

1. Land

It isn't possible to construct an off-grid dwelling without having enough land for it. Real estate accounts for large proportions of the costs involved in launching this type of lifestyle, with lots of individuals choosing to buy properties and construct rather than change the existing structure. You can, however, purchase an apartment that is disconnected from the grid, but it could cost you hundreds of thousands, or many thousands.

2. Off-grid solar system

A brand-new solar panel off grid can cost anything from $45,000 to $65,000, based upon the amount of electricity that you require (pre rebates tax credits, tax credits or incentives from the state). The more power you need to supply your home with power the greater this figure is, so when your house is bigger or you have more residents living there You'll likely have to pay more.

3. Private well

A private well drilling cost about $5,500 that's $15 to $30 per foot. However, this could increase if the soil isn't suitable to be used for digging.

4. Septic system

Between $10,000 and around $25,000 is the average price of an entire septic system that includes a leach field as well as a tank and pipe. There are alternatives for composting toilets, like those that have greywater systems, however they require more effort (and they may not be less expensive also).

Backup generators, off grid house insurance, and the costs associated to your heating system regardless of whether it's gas or diesel-powered stove, wood-burning stove or another heating method is something you should take into consideration.

The above costs don't mean that getting off the grid is costly. When you're considering selling your house and relocating without grid electricity and relocating to a different location, the price could be similar or even less than buying an entirely new house that's not completely off the grid. But when one of your primary goals is to shift towards a more affordable way of life, you must be aware of your budget and know what you're getting yourself into.

What are the reasons to get off the GRID?

We're constantly asked about why we are in a remote area by family members, friends or even by strangers.

Why do we have to endure the hassle of carrying wood, pumping water from lakes and having to deal with generators that will not start if we live without electricity? Why not reside in a city that provides everything you need? You wouldn't have to think about producing electricity, heat or water off the grid.

Are you thinking about leaving the grid? Though your motives might differ from ours, here are a couple of thoughts that pop into your the mind of those who ask why we do what we do.

1. to be self-sufficient

One of the main reasons we opted to leave the grid was the ability to depend on ourselves the most possible. This was probably the reason that prompted me to quit banking and create my own writing business as a freelancer. I wanted to take control of my finances.

The reason why we are off the grid is because we are worried with the future. In this way, we are more comfortable making sure we are taking care of our energy needs using solar energy and a battery storage.

Regarding living in a homestead, ensuring our food sources, and decreasing our dependence on propane to power our home systems as well as generator fuel however, we're far from where we'd like to be.

2. ENERGY INDEPENDENCE OF GRID

We experienced numerous power outages while living in the metropolis in the east in the beginning of 2000. I began to worry more about what my family's situation would be when the power of the city went out for a prolonged period. Particularly during the sometimes severe Canadian winters.

It's time to confront the facts. I was somewhat anxious about the process of generating our power and providing our water and heat. Additionally, I had no prior knowledge of off-grid electricity and water pumping in the winter months, or working with batteries.

Why are you interested in Off-Grid Living?

If you're thinking of changing to an off-grid home consider the reasons you'd like to do this. Here are a few of the most popular reasons we're hearing:

to become more self-sufficient

to stay completely off the grid

to help you save money,

to be more in touch with the natural world to feel more connected to nature

to get away from people

the problem

Think about how self-sufficient you would like to be in terms energy.

Be as specific as you can. Remember that no two off-grid living styles are the same.

Certain people, like want to be away from others. However, we love being surrounded by neighbors. One of our best family members lives on the other side of the road.

Who's completely off the grid these days?

As interest in self-sufficientand sustainable communities rises as concerns over the European continent's dependence on imported gas increase more people are looking to go "off-grid."

Many thousands of people are waiting on lists to get innovative eco-friendly eco-villages built by pioneering businesses. The technology of today is more advanced and more efficient or more affordable, making eco-friendly homes possible for those with the money to afford the cost. However, has technology improved enough to allow it to be feasible for everyone else?

Grids function as centralized networks that provide energy to the areas required in our electricity and gas delivery infrastructures. Grids often purchase surplus renewable energy from consumers to ensure it's full-charged during periods of low energy as well as demand and supply are closely and matched.

The act of detaching from the grid is leaving the safety net behind, that has been a challenge for people who wish to live off grid. If the sun wasn't shining or the wind was not blowing living off grid required a substantial reduction in energy usage. Today, as technology for energy storage has improved to the point that we can save excess gusts and rays to be used in calmer and dark periods, instead of selling the excess electricity back to grids, we are able to keep excess rays and gusts to be used in the calmer and darker times. Although, once storage issues have been solved, the question of whether we are able to produce enough energy.

Utilizing a range of options is crucial to generating enough energy to be able to live in a non-grid environment. The amount of energy used by the typical family is different according to where they live. For instance, on US mainland, the average usage is approximately 30 kilowatts per day however in Hawaii the usage is just the half. Heating homes consumes much energy in colder regions such as the UK in which the average household uses around 100-kilowatts of energy per day.

There are, however, various ways to keep warm, the simplest one being to use biomass (wood and other organic material). It is possible to collect the natural heat of the environment for heating water system with solar thermal collectors or ground heat pumps that are source-based. These are expensive to buy, costing a few thousands of dollars, but they're efficient and, as an investment over the long term investment they will be able to pay for themselves within a couple of years. The cooking oils that are left over can be transformed into eco-friendly biodiesel that can be used for heating oil or as a fuel for cars.

Off grid for our gas can possibly help us deal with two problems at the same time. Businesses are making the most of our waste including dog poop, to the famous London fatberg and you could also. Food waste, waste water, and sewage can be transformed into fuel to cook your food using an at-home anaerobic digester. For a price of PS700 the savings generated on gas generated would require a long time to recuperate, but it's an effective method to generate biogas and fertilizer, while dealing with the waste.

It's a lot more difficult to meet the electricity needs of our modern lives regardless of where we are. Solar power is currently the most preferred option with the typical solar system costing around PS8,000 to power a typical UK home. You can make money in just eight years, if you take the cost of maintenance. For the typical family, wind makes less sense. A rooftop-mounted turbine produces only a quarter the 45,000 kilowatt hours used by UK families each year however, if you have enough space to install a 6-kW turbine, it'll cost you at least PS20,000, and it could require the entire lifetime of the turbine to cover the cost.

Is going off the grid an acceptable alternative? If you decide to go off grid, you'll have the option of using the combination of storage and technology. The cost of getting off grid and creating this kind of freedom is costly for the majority of us. The best solution is to make a small switch away from grid dependence. When you've got between PS5,000 to PS8,000 available solar PV makes the most sense since it offers the fastest payback and can be further enhanced by wood-burning energy, particularly in the event that you can negotiate cheap solar panels as well as the wood.

It is all within our reach to decrease our dependence on the grid simply by making use of less energy. Our current energy use is extremely inefficient - and there are some ways we can alter our habits today to make off grid living more practical and reduce our energy costs, regardless of whether or not we're off grid.

The process of changing one's habits

Reduce the temperature The most energy-intensive energy uses within our homes is the heating of water. Just lowering the thermostat one degree can save about 10% off your heating bills.

Reducing the energy used by lighting: Around 15% of electricity in residential homes is used to light. You should consider switching to LED lighting which can be up to 90 percent higher efficiency than conventional bulbs. The savings can be recovered in as little as just a few months.

Changes in the way the clothes are dried and washed could yield substantial savings. Making the switch to cold water could reduce up to 90 percent of the energy used for washing clothes (most cleaning products are specifically designed to function at low temperatures) and drying your clothes in a natural manner whenever feasible could save about the same amount of power as cleaning them, and remove the requirement to use intensive and energy-intensive ironing.

Conserve and store the heat that you produce. Through tackling drafts by installing loft insulation you could stop as much as 25% of the heat in your home from venting through the roof. Even better, isolate yourself. Our homes are currently four degrees cooler than they were fifty years ago. Instead I'm reaching out for a second blanket of clothes.

Living without electricity could be a possibility, however it's not as cheap as you'd think. Renewable energy sources like wind, solar biomass, biomass, and even biogas are an option. But the reduction of energy use and waste can allow you to travel farther. With the present condition of battery storage, as well as other technology and as living off grid is becoming more popular It won't take long before more people are able to afford it with less expense.

Things to Know Before You disconnect from the grid (SA as an example)

Being a resident of South Africa has one major advantage: we receive plenty of suns! Sun power that makes use of the sun's energy to create electricity, is great for the environment as well as the cost of electricity. But, it could take a while before you can see a profit for your money. You may not have enough money available in the present. Credit is the way to enter the picture. When properly used credit such as Capitec's Access Facility can assist you in achieving your goal of living without grid, while also saving money in the long run. Here are five things you should consider before you go solar.

1. Your appliances and lights

You'll have to change your lighting prior to changing to solar energy. Switch your light bulbs to LED bulbs if you haven't already done it. LED bulbs help you kill two birds with one stone. They can help you save money in power consumption and also reduce how much solar power that you'll need.

Electric appliances consume a significant amount of energy as well. It is a good idea to upgrade your stove and heater by gas for those who want to stay away from the grid.

2. How much space are you allowed to use?

Solar power systems require an enormous amount of space. In the beginning, you'll require around 20 solar panels which are easily installed in the roofing. In addition, you'll need an internal space to store your batteries. It could take between 30 and 30 batteries dependent on the size of the installation.

3. Maintenance continues.

While solar systems for power are low-maintenance in their operation, they do require attention, particularly solar panels. They can get dirty over time, decreasing their efficiency. Fortunately, cleaning them generally solves the issue. Although the panels will are durable they'll likely need replacements every 25-40 years, which is expensive.

If you're using batteries, it is necessary to replace them often. The most recent models are available and tend to last longer than older models. "Lithium batteries need to be replaced every 8-10 years, with a particular focus on the regions that are hotter in our country. Common deep cycle solar batteries, like calcium, lead as well as others AGM (absorbed glass mat) batteries, are able to recharge between 1500 and 2 500 times. "These old-fashioned batteries must be replaced every 3 to five times," explains Paul Lombard of Regenergy the energy solutions firm.

4. Your contingency plan

If you plan to live completely without electricity, bear in mind its limits. If your solar energy system is damaged for any reason, ensure that you have a backup power source installed so that you won't be being left without power while it's being fixed.

5. The hidden costs

There are some hidden costs to keep in mind. If you're off the grid, there are two kinds of Small-Scale Embedded Generation (SSEG) systems are commonly used Grid-tied SSEG systems as well as off-grid, as well as standalone SSEG systems.

Grid-connected SSEG system makes sure that you're continuously connected to power grid of your city. It is required to pay a monthly or daily service fee, as well as the energy cost per kWh, however should you generate excess power, you'll be able to get the cash back. The account you have will get charged at a feed-in cost for any excess electricity that you put back into the grid. Since not all municipalities offer this service, you'll need to contact the office in your area to find out the extent of any hidden charges.

It is also possible to opt for an unfeed-in PV system that is tied to the grid to prevent any surplus electricity generated on your home from getting fed back to the grid.

You'll require an off-grid or an independent SSEG system that is completely away from the grid. These systems are physically separate from grid power in addition to being electrically isolated.

What will going off the grid costs in SA?

Beginning a business is expensive. Estimates of the cost to get away from the grid can are ranging between R150 000 up to R350 000, based on the requirements of your use. There is however positive news. It's not necessary to invest all in the first day You can make the transition to solar at any the course of time.

The application process to our access facility can represent the initial step towards leaving the grid. according to your information, you could be granted an amount of credit at least R250 000. This is a low-cost line credit that places you in control due to:

You decide the amount and frequency you can borrow is available from the access facility you have to use.

In the end that you can use as many or as little in your limit of credit as would like.

In the event that your finances has changed you can simply alter your repayment amount or duration or time, and the amount you've repaid is available.

Anybody who meets the criteria is eligible to apply to our access facility and you don't need to make a bank account with us in order in order to apply. Bring your valid SA ID as well as a smart ID (new customers only) as well as your three consecutive pay slips to a Capitec branch (you must be employed for a continuous period of time). Additionally, you'll need an official bank statement that has the three most recent deposit of your salary on it (only when your wages are not being paid to the Capitec bank account).

Fire Skills off the grid

7 Creative Ways to light a fire without using matches

Fire is a singular nature phenomenon which has formed the human race. Our forefathers attained some influence on nature taking control of the powerful genie.

However, without the technological innovations in the making of fires that humans have created, like lighters and matches that we have, we're not better off than the people who were living centuries ago. The ability to start an open flame in the wild could be the crucial difference between life and death.

Collect the following items into separate piles prior to trying to start a fire:

1. Tinder can be described as a dry and easily combustible substance that can be ignited by one or two sparks. Plant material that is soft and fibrous may be used to make an tinder. Tinder could also be very fine steel wool. Although tinder is able to quickly catch fire, it isn't able to continue to burn.

2. Kindling is a tad thicker organic material that is used to fuel a fire which has been ignited with an igniter. Kindling is made of dried wood chippings, small twigs, or the dry stalks of grass.

3. Firewood: Bigger logs and twigs require longer time before they reach the beginning point, but once ignited they maintain the fire for a longer time.

Let's take a look at seven ways to start a fire to increase your survival skills after you've learned the basics.

1. Method of hand drilling

Let's start by introducing the most basic method. This is the longest-lasting method to start fires however the benefit is that you don't require any special equipment or chemicals.

To make a fireboard you'll require a sturdy piece of wood. With a knife or pointed pebble, make an opening in the. In order to fit this notch you'll require a stick that is two feet long. When you roll this stick, also known as a spindle in between the palms of your hands, you'll be able to roll in the direction of the notch, and generate heat via friction. It will heat up enough to begin smoking, and produce small sparks over time.

The tinder should be blown out to stimulate the flame as you capture the flames. Inject a few sparking slivers. You can build it up further by adding bigger pieces of wood.

2. Bow drill method

Since you can drill faster and last longer without arousing your hands it is a more efficient version of hand-drilling. A piece or rock can be used hold the spindle within the notch on the fireboard. Bend a stick that is stout and secure the ends by using a string for bows.

The bow can be operated using just one hand, by wrapping the string once around the spindle and then turning the spindle in a circular motion. The second hand is used to press downwards on the stone that is on the top of the spindle increasing the frictional heat generated.

Once you've got the hang of it, the drilling process will accelerate, getting closer to the goal quicker, as indicated by flaming embers and smoke. As the tinder begins to smell, begin to build your fire with blowing, and adding fuel.

3. By using an engineered fire plough

A back-andforth motion is utilized for creating friction between spindle and the fireboard rather than the drill technique employed in previous techniques. To make a fireboard long piece of wood is utilized. You can create a groove across all the way to the end, stopping below the edge. This can be accomplished with the penknife or rock.

The spindle should be moved between the groove. Leave a little amount of tinder on the edge. You should sit with your legs stretched out with the distal end of the fireboard firmly held in between the feet. The proximal portion should be propped against an object between your legs, creating some slope. If you lean onto the spindle as you move it you'll be able to make use of the full upper body instead of your hands. Make sure that the tinder is ignited and the fire has been constructed as it was.

4. Steel and the flint

Steel sets and flint ready-made are available to purchase and should be part of each survival kit. Flint is a gray-colored stone with a somewhat smooth surface. If you don't have it then search for pieces. The second alternative is a quartz stone that can be distinguished from its sparkling glass-like surface. Gather several stones and hit every one using a small piece iron or a knife. The sparks that come from the iron will cause the fire to sputter and smoke aiding you in starting the fire.

5. A glowing mirror or a glass

Let's borrow a page from Archimedes' work and emulate his style of. If he could ignite the entire fleet of vessels by directing sunrays onto the ships from afar, then igniting sparks in a nearby tinder is a piece of cake. When you were in school you may have smuggled grass or paper with the aid of a magnifying lens.

The brand new Mini Pocket Power Plus can recharge all of your electronic devices and help you jump-start your car!

To remove it you'll require an asymmetric mirror or lens. The reflector of a flashlight or the side of a toothpaste-polished can be used. The lens can be constructed from the clear container that is that is filled with water.

The aim is to concentrate light on a specific spot until the substance has reached the temperature at which it ignites. Did you realize that the Olympic torch still burns the same way at Olympia, Greece, where it started? The hardest part is obtaining enough light to meet your objective.

6. Steel wool and battery

To light an ignition in the present time, you can use the flashlight battery along with a tiny amount of steel wool. It is massaged on the battery contacts until it begins to smolder. Once the steel wool has burned completely, the fire should be transferred immediately to the fire tinder.

7. Combustion using chemical methods

As our final practice We'll move between chemistry and physics and end with a bang. Literally. Since this chemical reaction creates flame with just two chemicals to create an explosive reaction it is important to remain in the distance from the event.

The crystals of potassium permanganate as well as glycerin will be required. When they are dissolved in water the former acts as a disinfectant. This makes it a valuable product to have within your emergency kit for cleansing water and cleaning wounds. Glycerin is a flavoring additive that is also an inactive ingredient in a variety of syrupy medicines. It's sold at drugstores and bakery supply shops.

Within the nest, put the either a leaf or paper using the equivalent of a teaspoon of potassium permanganate. Sit back and drop couple of drops of glycerin on the crystals. After a short time an explosion of a tiny size will take place, which will ignite your spark.

However when you attempt to ignite an fire, make sure you have the right tools to extinguish it. Use all of the normal fire safety precautions as well. A well-controlled fire has substantial benefits, whereas uncontrolled fires can cause havoc.

Retrieving and Purifying Water

Are you interested in knowing how to get clean water, even If you live away from the main road?

In the modern age it is essential to have a safe and reliable source of clean drinking water is crucial and when you decide to depart from the typical urban life style and have electricity and other necessities, you have to be able to account for water. It is essential to have a secure and ample supply of drinkable water.

Living off the grid does not require sacrificing your comforts at home or even security however, when getting clean drinking water isn't as easy as turning on the faucet and water source. Storage, water and use are an increasingly complicated process. There are many alternatives for you to choose from.

Removing Water from the Grid

Most people don't realize of the variety different off-grid sources of water. The options are varied dependent on where you reside However, you might be interested in creating an off-grid dwelling close to water sources. These are the most sought-after water sources for those who are off grid.

1. WELLS

The most common source of water that is suitable for living off grid is water wells. The drilling of a well within the United States costs about $5,500 in the average, and they're typically at about 150 feet in depth. It becomes more costly as the well becomes deep, but when it's completed, you'll have a steady source of water that's also low maintenance.

Your well's depth is determined by your water table. The water table can be about 100 feet beneath the surface in areas that are more humid However, in dry or desert environments it is possible to dig up to 1000 feet. Excavating and drilling an underground well is a long-lasting procedure, so make sure you be sure to research the process in case you're considering a well for your property.

Additionally, you'll need pumps to get the water out of your well. Pumps are either manual, similar to traditional wells you've seen in stories, or electrical as well as solar powered. Water collection is more efficient with the right pump.

It's also important to note that wells shouldn't be used in earthquake-prone areas or in areas in which hydraulic fracking is prevalent because a single act could mean the end of your hard-earned money and the water supply.

2. RAINWATER

The region you reside in and the infrastructure you have to store rainwater, relying on rainwater is an unwise choice. Rainwater is neither cost nor easy to gather. It is a fantastic source if you are in an area that experiences moderate to high levels of rainfall. Rainwater is also among the most pure sources of water naturally occurring.

The investment in a rain-water catchment system will allow you to transfer water through your roofing into a storage. It is possible to determine the amount of water you'll be in a position to collect through this method. With every inch rain every square foot of roof area will be able to capture 0.623 grams of water. The only thing you require is the square footage of your roof and the information on local rainfall for the area you live in to form your estimates. You'll be amazed at how much water you could collect and store. It could reduce the need for costly water sources.

The rain-collection systems suitable for certain roof types, particularly slate or metal. The rainwater drainage on roofs made of asphalt isn't efficient and drinking it could be dangerous. Prior to drinking water from rain, it is important to consider how it has was treated and filtered.

3. SPRINGS

Freshwater is found in springs that naturally form, however, they're not very common. If you're lucky enough to be near one, it's recommended to use it to supply your water. Springs are completely free and provide large amounts of water, based on their dimensions. Springs are nature's answer for wells made by humans, since they develop as groundwater rises and then flows into the surface via fractures in the earth.

A small percentage of people have the privilege of having an aqueduct running through their off-grid land. When you begin looking for the perfect plot, you'll discover that plots with access to springs are considerably more costly.

Be aware that using an natural source of water leaves you at the mercy to the conditions. A dry winter could mean that you don't have the same access to spring water as you normally do, and your pipes might be frozen during winter.

4. PONDS and RIVERS

For centuries, naturally moving water is a reliable source. However, you might not be able use this water as easily as you think in the present world. In many states, the use of streams, rivers, and ponds is illegal. The proper Water Rights must be considered in Western states. This is simply saying that even if the water is situated on one of your properties, you don't be entitled to utilize it. You could face penalties if you drink water from the nature-based source.

The Purchase of water off the Grid

Off-grid living is supposed to signify freedom from the shackles of urban infrastructure. The purchase of water and the transportation back to your residence is against this principle, however it's entirely possible. Many off-grid dwellings depend on the purchase of water and are usually purchased through an enormous water tank which can be pulled behind or carried in the vehicle.

The purchase of water signifies that you are dependent to the grid in a certain way for your survival and, consequently, it sabotages the desire to live an off-grid lifestyle. It's also expensive, and if you're running in water shortage at an unavoidable time, you'll have no option but to wait until you are able to purchase more. Water purchases in bulk aren't always feasible, which is why it's a possibility you decide to save until last.

Off-Grid Water Supply

People who live off grid would like to live a lifestyle as similar to their old one as is possible. This means the availability of running water in their off-grid homes. This is feasible due to two main systems.

The original system has been in use for quite a while and operates by moving water through your pipes through gravity. The gravity-fed storage method is easy to set up, and the water will flow through the pipes for as long as your tank is situated above your home. The drawbacks of this method are the difficulties of raising your water tank to a sufficient height in the absence of a rain collection system installed. You can choose to pump manually or mechanically water into the tank, which could take a lengthy time.

Motorized pumps are another option to provide the water you need to run your house. Solar-powered pumps are offered for powered pumps which provide water pressure to your home. Pumps are available in a range of flow rates and are able to offer strong pressure for water as required.

Alternatives for Water Storage

Water tanks are required to keep the water you store secure and easily available, which we've discussed. If you're in an area that is not connected to the grid, you'll almost always require lots of water. Spring water and rainwater typically require the installation of a cistern. This is a different term for a water tank, however it is usually known as underground tanks.

Tanks made of plastic are among the most popular tanks, however they can be made from any kind of material, and stone, metal, and cement cisterns being seen in numerous off-grid communities. Due to its strength and resistance to microbial and microbe growth it is the most commonly used option. As mentioned previously that elevating the water tank could help in reducing water pressure through allowing gravity to transfer the water throughout your system.

Remediation and Filtration of Off Grid Water

Locating a reliable source of water and the storage of it are the two most important steps to making sure that you're getting a constant supply of water. However, you must also take into consideration its security. Since virtually any water source that is natural may be contaminated and you'll require some kind of water purifier or treatment device. While some sources of water are more clean than others filtering or an treatment system is recommended for total happiness and tranquility.

An inline or gravity-fed water filtering method is the most effective option to treat the water that is off grid. Gravity-fed filters are a low-cost solution that's also simple to maintain. They don't require plumbing, and are perfect when you're in search of an easy, yet effective method to purify the water that comes from off-grid sources to ensure it is healthy to consume.

The water you choose to cook or consume and the water you want to wash with, must be treated or filtered. There are many situations when the use of untreated water is acceptable, such as:

Garden watering is so long as the fruits and vegetables are washed and thoroughly cleaned prior to consumption.

When it comes to washing,

When you use an antibacterial or disinfectant soap clean your hands.

Showering is safe so it is not accompanied by bleeding wounds or water sucked up.

Animals and pets should be cleaned as they are less prone to infections caused by water than humans.

It's your choice what you do with the water filtration process, but any water that is consumed or absorbed by your body should be protected by a system to protect the body.

Don't Forget your Waste Water

What will happen to water that you collected and treated after having utilized it? There are two kinds of waste water that you can use:

Greywater can be recycled, and is derived from sinks, washing machines tubs, showers, and tubs.

Blackwater is a waste product from toilets that needs to be eliminated or properly treated.

A specifically-designed blackwater treatment system like compost toilets or septic tank, can be used by the majority of off-grid homeowners. This ensures that this type of garbage is treated in a safe manner and kept from our water sources. Toilets with composting are less popular than conventional septic tanks however, they are believed to be more sustainable and last longer.

Greywater can be utilized in many ways around your home for storage, as well as correctly making use of to water your yard. The water should first be treated and then kept in an additional tank. It is then possible to select the right treatment or filter that meets your requirements. Greywater treatment machines that filter the water through, allowing it to be used safely for gardening are available.

The choices for managing wastewater could be restricted by the location you live in as certain restrictions or rules could limit your options. Once you've identified your options, you can select the best option for your house.

Off-Grid Water Systems to suit your lifestyle and needs

A myriad of personal preferences will determine which system of water is the best for your off-grid life. It is possible that you have an off-grid house equipped with a full rain collection system, or be blessed with access to fresh water sources. Or, you may start from scratch and seeking the best piece of land for your dream home on.

A variety of factors can influence the decision you make to go off grid If you're looking to live as simple as you can, you might not want to think about the extensive process of drilling your wells or associated activities. However, relying solely on rain collection systems may not be the ideal solution when you reside in an area that has a low rainfall.

The final decision you make will be affected by the budget you have set and your geographic place. This is a choice worth thinking over, especially if aren't sure if you've yet purchased your property. As you can see in the above list there are a number of options for bringing water from the outside to your home.

Gardening off-grid at the most fundamental level

Three Easy Steps to Self-Sustaining Off-Grid Garden

For hundreds of years, civilizations across the globe have been able to sow, produce and harvested crops using only local resources and work. This changed around the time of the 1950s. The introduction of hybrid plants, along with synthetic fertilizers, as well as potent chemical insecticides, were developed. These innovations altered the plant's natural ecosystem by replacing it with a sterilized, chemically-dependent system.

Despite modern gardening practices It is still possible to create a sustainable garden by retracing the steps of the past. The sustainable garden can only benefit through the involvement of the homestead.

Sunlight, water, soil seeds, pest and disease control are the five most important components. This article focuses on the final three elements that we've previously discussed, such as selecting the most suitable location for sunlight and water.

1. Improved Soil

The soil which has been amended has the addition of nutrients in order to ensure healthy growth for plants. The amount of amendments needed is contingent upon several variables that include the initial amount of nutrients, the development history, and the plant concentration.

I suggest using French intense or square-foot garden strategies previously mentioned on Off The Grid News for the long-term maintenance of your garden. The basic idea is that plants are grown close to the soil and in a rich. Since the soil is well composted, it occupies less space, but it creates more. Also, water usage is reduced to a minimum which is essential for any homestead.

Consider that 2 cubic yards of compost are needed for each 100 square feet of garden. While this might not seem to be a lot experts in the field know the amount of raw material needed to make the two cubic feet compost that has been cured.

Compost can be created using different ways however, they generally belong to two types: plants-based and animal-based. The best choice is determined by the homestead's activities. We'll examine three possible options here.

a) Green manure

Cover crops are plants in the garden prior to or after the crops that produce food. They help protect soil from erosion and also providing essential nutrients to the future plants.

Green manure is the term used to describe the cover crops that are cultivated in your garden. They are then returned to the soil while it is still green. Cover crops, usually planted in the fall , after the summer harvest has been completed it allows for some growth prior to winter. The cover crop could die in the winter months or become dormant only to return to life in the spring, based on the variety of crop being sown. Winter rye is a good choice to plant in autumn in an area to be used to grow the summer crop. This is tilled (or manually dug) to the ground in the early spring after it has come into life. The soil that has been modified is perfect for squash, tomatoes and other summer favourites when the frost date is the most recent.

In winter, plant winterkilling crop varieties in areas that can be used to grow spring crops. Non-dormant wheat is a good illustration. When the soil is working in spring, the wheat can be tilled into soil which means that your garden is prepared for the spring crop.

B) Compost Crops

Another option is to grow vegetables that are harvested , and then the organic matter decays in compost piles. The advantage of compost crops (also called carbon-rich crops) can be that they can frequently be used as fodder or food. Sorghum, wheat and corn are examples of grain which can be processed by individuals or fed to animals. The plants that remain are composted after the grains are harvested and the compost that has been cured is later placed in the garden.

C) Animal Compost

The compost crops are able to be used to replace or enhanced with manure from animals from rabbits, chickens cattle and other animals that are vegetarian. Animal dung, as with compost made of plants, has to be treated. Homesteaders with plenty of manure just sprinkle it over gardens in autumn (after the harvest of the summer crops) to let it dry through the winter. Your garden is ready for be used by the time spring arrives.

2. Seeds and plants

Seed saving is crucial for a green garden, whether your garden is for human consumption, compost or fodder.

Hybrids are the mainstay of seeds that are sold in catalogs, and they are the main reason for seedlings are sold in nurseries. There is no way to grow hybrid seeds because the plants are always inferior even though they produce greater quantities of crops and can be resistant to diseases.

3. Control of diseases and pests

Organically grown gardens and without the application of synthetic fertilizers or pesticides that are toxic are healthy for the soil. The most effective protection against diseases and pests is a healthy ecosystem.

But, even a healthy ecosystem could be a victim of diseases or pests. Three additional methods can help reduce the loss of plants caused by diseases or pests.

For starters, crop rotation is a must. Pests that are naturally apprehensive become confused after returning to the spot next year only to find that their favorite plant isn't since the crops are planted at different places each year.

Companion plant, on the contrary is an extremely efficient tool. Many plants work in tandem to increase development and to keep pests away. Radishes are a good example. scattered over the squash patches, can deter squash insects.

In the end, picking bugs by hand can be a viable alternative. Hornworms for example are a source of negative effects on tomatoes. This can be reduced by eliminating them from the plants. Though labor-intensive and inefficient this is an acceptable option for small gardens.

Why is it beneficial to live off the grid? to your mental well-being?

As per the National Alliance on Mental Illness One in five American has a mental health issue every year. The reasons are many however the ubiquity of technology and media along with the absence of a sense of sense of purpose in modern society has been identified as the main causes. As the 180,000 currently off-grid American families can attestto, living off grid can improve mental well-being by restoring the feeling of self-confidence motivation, purpose, and empowerment we all seem to be lacking. While living off-grid can be stressful and difficult at times, you're ultimately responsible for the results. Your mental health will naturally improve when you can count on your strengths and resources to tackle problems.

1. You'll feel better by eating a balanced diet.

An increasing amount of research suggests that the standard American diet is associated with poor mental well-being. A lot of Americans consume processed foods that contain harmful chemicals like refined sugar and trans fats as well as synthetic colorings, additives and other chemicals. These substances have been proven to cause harm to the brain in a variety of occasions. The people who consumed the highest amount of processed sugar (17 teaspoons per day, which is approximately two cans of Coca-Cola) had a 23 per cent higher risk be diagnosed with depression or anxiety in the next five years than people who ate under 10 teaspoons per day according to a new study on the effects of sugar intake on mood. It is possible to anticipate growing and eating a wide selection of fresh diet that is healthy organic and free of chemicals once you are off the grid.

Your healthy diet will enhance not just your physical health, but your emotional and psychological health and help you better manage the daily demands of self-sufficiency.

2. Self-Responsibility can be strengthened by living Off the Grid

The modern world is expected to trust certain established institutions to lead their lives. With real power at the disposal of business and government Many people are stuck at jobs that they don't enjoy and this naturally triggers feelings of despair, anxiety as well as melancholy, worry and stress. Living off-grid can help you get rid of a stale life and a dependence. You are able to regain control over your life, and completely rely on yourself for your survival and happiness. Your mental health will improve drastically as a result this conviction. The people who believed their lives had meaning for instance and were able to reduce by 15% their probability of dying within 14 years over those who were unable to find a purpose in their lives, as per one study.

Off-grid living permits you to be engaged in meaningful work every day which boosts your happiness and overall well-being. This means that your cortisol levels are reduced which is beneficial to brain function and immune control which improves physical and mental wellbeing.

3. Connection To Nature

Living off grid requires much time in the outdoors and tending to your garden. Being in the natural world has been proven to increase your overall health.

The participants in a research study conducted at the University of British Columbia were divided into three categories which included those who took part in activities that were connected to the natural world (such as going for walks or looking at plants) as well as those who observed the creation of man as well as those who did neither. Happiness, a feeling of elevated status, and a sense of connection to others (not just the natural world) were significantly more prevalent for the former group than the other groups.

Gardening every day is a calming and therapeutic exercise that permits you to process your feelings instead of just burying them. It is always recommended to tackle difficult or turbulent emotions when you're struggling dealing with your emotions. If you're away from the city and have no electricity, you'll also have the liberty to go outdoors when you're in need of processing your emotions in a positive efficient way.

4. Mind Clarity and Peace

Crowds, noise, pollution traffic, noise, and intrusive technology all add to the sensory oversaturation that modern life brings. In the end, it's not a surprise that anxiety and disorientation are commonplace. A lot of us have a difficult time separating our thoughts and attain peace and tranquility within our hectic world.

When you are in a place that is not connected to the grid you're always able to find the time to reflect and connection to your inner self. Off grid living is at an accelerated pace, and requires attention and patience. Simply focus on the job at hand and ensure that the task is done correctly. This means that your mind is tuned out by unwanted or negative thoughts, which restores mental harmony and health.

If you have pets to take care of as well as a garden to take care of and an endless list of chores that need to be done it's likely that you'll feel happier, more content and fulfilled in your life. Being off the grid helps you escape from your mind and break through any negative thinking patterns that you may be experiencing. It's all about learning new skills and meeting objectives, which will boost the self-confidence and happiness of your.

Animal Care off-grid

Based on The Mother Nature Network, an area of half-acre is usually large enough to accommodate people and animals who live away from the grid. The maintenance of the property takes lots of effort and those who decide to live off grid also have to take care of their pets, themselves or animals. To ensure that your pets get the best treatment while also decreasing or eliminating your dependence to the grid it is essential to plan and implement an animal-friendly strategy that is focused on animal welfare. These guidelines will aid you in reaching your goals.

Solar energy is a great source for keeping animals cozy throughout the season long.

If you have pets that live outdoors all year it is essential to ensure they are warm. Because the climate varies and you'll have to consider the seasons and plan according to the season. The creation of (or changing) heated barns that are solar powered for livestock is among the most effective methods in keeping your animals warm and dry outside of the home. Horse stables, dog houses and other off-grid facilities are all able to benefit from solar panels. When it is hot solar panels could be used to provide fans to ensure that animals stay cool and clean.

Be aware that the majority users of solar panels aren't completely off grid. They typically make use of a mix of solar and grid energy. Technology advancements have allowed them to eliminate connections with local utility companies. The most important thing to do this safely and without risking the comfort of your pets and their well-being is to ensure you have enough battery storage capacity when installing an solar-powered system.

How to Turn Your Dog into an Active Dog

Blue heelers are great to herd livestock in areas that are off grid.

Dogs are smart and loyal animals. They are wonderful companions and even help their owners in non-grid environments. When you train your loyal dog to be a work dog, he could assist in taking care of your pets. You can also train them to defend themselves against intruders. If you're planning to put your dog in the field then you must be sure to treat him with respect to protect your pets and for the safety of your property. This means providing rewards such as rewards, praise, and playing. It is not advisable to use aggression to teach your dog. It can take time for working dogs to be accustomed to performing tasks on farms.

If you don't have dogs, be thinking about the breed prior to purchasing one. Certain breeds are more adept in guarding and herding more than others. Australian shepherds border collies, collies are dogs that are famous for their capacity to collect animals. The Australian shepherd is a ideal choice if you're focused on the guarding aspect. Along with herding well they also guard with a ferociousness. The Doberman Pinscher is a wonderful breed of guard dog to think about in the event that you aren't planning to keep animals.

Help Your Animals Defend Against predators

Also, you'll need to ensure that your pets are safe from any predators that may be in the vicinity. Coyotes are known to leap to incredible heights, and fences that are as high as eight feet might be required to ensure the safety of animals. Livestock require secure pens that they return after their grazing the fields. Use a cloth made of hardware to keep predators smaller than a dog out of chicken coops. This includes weasels.

Start putting together a pet health plan as soon as you can.

You can effectively take care of your animals off grid by using solar panels and batteries to cool or heat sheds to house your animals and transform your dog to a animal, as well as also keep your pets protected from predators. The trick to doing it right is to prepare in advance and then implement your plan efficiently and in a timely way. You'll be on the path towards self-sufficiency for animals and pets if adhere to the guidelines in this article now.

Chapter 2: Alternative Energy Off The Grid

Alternative Power Sources to Live Off the GridThe possibility to live a more sustainable life by using alternative sources of power is now the norm as technological advances continue to create new forms of green and clean energy sources.

Geothermal, solar, wind hydropower, and solar power make it possible for people to be "off from the grid" that is, where the use of renewable energy sources and natural power is a better alternative to conventional power sources. Natural power off-grid power source inventions come in a range of shapes and sizes dependent on whether you reside in a remote area or you want to reduce your energy costs.

1. Systems for Solar Energy

Off-grid power systems operate without the need for power lines. The energy they produce can be utilized for powering appliances. Off-grid solar systems is an example of this, and is solely powered by sun's energy for powering the appliances of the system. A hybrid off-grid, however is one that uses a combination of hydro, solar and wind energy as the main energy source.

A variety of alternative solar system setups can be found based on the kind of power that is required (AC or DC voltage). In spite of the energy output the majority of systems utilize sunlight energy in the same method. Solar panels are among the most commonly used techniques for harvesting solar energy.

Solar panels are composed of a variety of photovoltaic cells that absorb the sun's energy and convert it to valuable electricity. Photovoltaic cells accomplish this by absorbing solar energy , and release electrons through semiconductors like silicon or Cadmium Telluride. Contacts made of metal to the panel's numerous surfaces transmit free electrons into one direction which result in the creation of a current. The final result is a currentthat is paired by the voltage that is stored inside the solar cells. This voltage is used to power electronic devices.

2. Hydroelectric Power Plants

The force generated by moving the water or falling is utilized to produce electricity in a hydroelectric power system. Large hydropower systems can generate enough energy to provide alternative energy to homes of millions and smaller hydropower systems are able to generate enough power to supply just one family.

There are many things that the majority of hydropower structures share regardless of size. The first step is to construct dams, which are basically a barrier that blocks an eddy of water from moving and raises the level of water, with the result is a miniature waterfall or controlled release of water on the opposite end that of the dam. The water accumulates an enormous amount of force when it flows across the dam. A turbine, which functions like a windmill is able to rotate as water moves the turbine's blades, turning the energy generated by it into mechanical power. The turbine is connected to a generator that turns when the turbine spins. It converts the mechanical power into electricity. In the end, electricity is transported through transmission lines which transfer it to homes and other devices. It is the amount produced by a hydroelectric power system will be determined by quantity of water that flows through it, as well as the distance that it travels.

3. Wind Turbines

Wind energy systems harvest the energy generated by wind and convert it into electrical or mechanical energy, like hydropower systems work. A wind turbine, that can be found in horizontal and vertical axes, is the most commonly used equipment used by wind systems.

Horizontal axis turbines are the most popular kind of wind turbine and is often used in large-scale wind systems that generate 100 Kilowatts or more. A nacelle, a rotor and a tower as well as certain electronic components are found in the majority of turbines.

If a wind turbine comes into contact with the wind, its rotors push the turbine in a similar way to the way that a hydroturbine relies on rotors in order to turn. Generator, that rotates together with the rotors located inside the nacelle. The nacelle, the rotor and electrical equipment are connected by the tower, which is used to feed the electricity produced by wind turbines to the power lines for utility use. A capacity of up to 5 000 kilowatts could be achieved dependent on how big the wind turbine.

Maintaining and Using Tools

The grid has been cut off. Your drill's battery is low. Maybe you'll be able get enough fuel to keep the generator in operation to power tools. Making investments on hand instruments that used to be popular in the past including the iconic hand drill that doesn't run on power might be a better idea.

1. 12-gauge shotgun

Use it to repel predators and to keep the rabbits from your garden area so that you can eat your vegetables as dinner.

2. Long-handle No. 2 round-point shovel

Dig a ditch. Extinguish the flame of a brush and cut through ice and snow. For the old no. 2 it's all the day's effort. Select a model with an extremely deep socket. This is the cup of metal at the top of the blade , which the handle slide into. It is almost indestructible because of this.

3. Cant hook

If you're planning to light an fire, you're likely need to move logs. If you employ one of these grabbers your back will last two times as long.

4. Chainsaw

Cut firewood using it and construct fence posts using it or cut down the fallen tree along your quarter-mile-long roadway.

5. Linesman pliers

These pliers are often referred to as side cutters due to the blades that are on their jaws can be used to do electrical repairs or cut fence wire as well as cut small screws and nails.

6. Framing hammer

If this heavier, larger version of a conventional clawhammer is approached the nail, it will fly away. Estwing's non-breakable solid-steel model is the best option.

7. An excellent knife

I'm not saying you should would like to purchase a multi-tool that comes with a myriad of additional features. Finding a good long, long pocketknife, however could be just what you require. An individual blade like those made by Opinel could go a long ways particularly since they're designed to be grippy when cutting.

8. Screwdriver

A screwdriver is an essential tool for fixing your shelter or home. A good one can last for a long time. They can be used as a screwdriver in addition to the chisel, however you may want to keep them separately. It's a great partner for drills. In the event of a crisis you can use it to cut the zombie.

9. Handsaws

A small set of unpowered saws, like hacksaws to cut metals, a carpenter's saw for wood and a keyhole saw for more precise details may be needed. There are also modular saws that look like hacksaws and feature blades that can be exchanged for various job.

10. Vice grip

A vice grip can be an extremely useful tool. It could be a grip or clamp, wrench, pliers and many more things in the pinch. In the event that your bag for bugouts is fast getting full it's best to carry equipment that can be utilized to serve a variety of purposes. Bonus points: A sturdy heavy, bulky one can be concealed in the sock to be use as weapons.

11. Bow and arrow

Even though guns aren't powered, it requires ammunition, gun oil and other things. A quality bow will last for a long time and even though you might be unable to find arrows when civilization is gone, it's simpler to make more than make new gun ammunition.

12. A Tarp

Ron Swanson would be proud of this spot in the listing. The tarp can serve as a blanket, shelter and barrier to quick-drying or even the water collection device.

13. Compass

In the modern age of GPS the art of compass seems to be almost lost, however should you have maps using a compass, it may be the best method to get away from danger zones towards higher elevations. It could also be an aid in retracing your steps, by recollecting the directions.

14. Duct tape

Duct tape has a humorous reputation among those who work at home and is a highly flexible tool when needed when it comes to the temporary sealing of pipes, repair or any other household tasks.

15. Rope

To build a fast but messy home, you can pair it with the use of a Tarp. Rope however is still a vital essential survival tool, whether it's used to secure the food supply from bears or wolves, drying clothing or binds an hunter. The best part is that it's generally reusable. If it breaks it can be repaired with a square knot that is a great way to fix it. In the event that you're using various kinds of rope it's best to improve knots.

16. Bike

Cars are prone to running out of fuel or malfunction in different ways. Although a bicycle can suffer from many issues but it's fairly simple to fix them all unlike the case of the latest model of car with more electronic components than mechanical ones. It might appear to be an instant escape option in the first place, but when you're trying to make it through the traffic jams, it appears more feasible. It's also more efficient than a machete-wielding criminal that is trying to chase your down.

The most common mistakes made by people living off grid.

Off-grid living is now an increasingly popular way of living. Many of us have thought about the appeal of leaving the hustle and bustle of urban life to peace and quiet for at the very least once. However, before you dive into the remote house with no internet connection be sure to read about the top 5 Common Off-Grid blunders and the best ways to avoid them:

FIRST MISTAKE: NOT BEING ABLE TO UNDERSTAND OTHER Power Sources

Do you think it is possible to go without electricity for the duration of an entire day? It's not a issue. Can you survive the darkness without electricity? This is a whole different matter. It might seem easy to swap your TV for an ebook and the dryer by a line but what happens if it's only 15 degrees at night, with no lights , and even worse there's no heating? Knowing how to harness sun's energy during the day and provide electricity at night is crucial to be able to live off the grid.

Do not do it: Prior to you turn off the power, learn the fundamentals.

Learn about solar panels inverters, charge panels generators, and battery banks from the bottom from the ground. Choose which one you'll use and learn how to make maximum benefit from it. Depending on the extent of off the grid you are and the location you live in, you might not have access to this advanced internet-connected equipment. There's no further instructions, so be aware of what you're doing prior to you start. Take a look at Off-Grid Solar for Dummies Basics for Beginners to help you get started.

Ignoring the fundamentals of gardening.

It may sound obvious It's not, but you'll be shocked at the difficulties to cultivate vegetables and fruits. Don't fall for the hype of your local farmer's market. It's not like they're well-groomed and ready to eat right out of the soil. Gardening can be a challenging job. Seeds, just like children, are very picky. Based on the seed, excessive or insufficient sunlight, a poor soil or excessive water are all contributing factors.

Beware of it by making a garden within your backyard.

You can study and read all you like, but the best method to become a successful gardener is to practice by doing. Choose a piece of land on your property and then play around with it over a couple of seasons. So, in the event that you do make a mistake on the path there won't be a situation of feast or famine when you're in the far reaches of the wilderness. Learn about the requirements for each seed and then refine it with trial and trial and. For beginners,

Vegetable Gardening is a fantastic beginning point.

MISTAKE #3: FAILING TO INSTALL A SUITABLE WASTE DISPOSAL SYSTEM.

Does it make sense for the bear to pee within the forest? Therefore, if you take your home off grid then you'll be out of the grid too. Furthermore that you don't have an effective disposal system could turn your perfect getaway into a hazard. This could result in contaminates in your food supply as well as drinking water, which can make your sick.

Beware of it by doing research on which method is the best one for you.

There are many garbage disposal options available. By doing a little research you'll be able to figure out which throne to be seated on. The decision you make will depend on the extent to which off the grid your plans are to get. Are you planning to use pit toilets or construct your own septic tank? Composting toilets can also assist you in turning your human waste into manure that you can use. It is the term used to describe a chain of foods. Take a look at the Off-Grid Sewage Guide to get the fundamentals.

4. Failure to be physically ready.

Get your hands dirty and let loose all of your Little House on the Prairie fantasiesbecause living off grid is manual labor on overdrive. There is no need to turn on heater and washing machines, dishwashers as well as other modern conveniences are gone. Being off the grid requires perseverance. Are you in the right physically to be cutting in the early hours of 5:30 a.m.? Perhaps, you could try running after the stray hens who fled in the middle of the night?

To prevent it from happening, start exercise as soon as possible.

It's not about your body shape; it's about protecting your life. To meet all the demands on your body from off grid chores, you should strengthen your upper and lower bodies. When you first start off off-grid This simple daily suggestion increases your chance of survival as well as reduce the chance of throwing your back in the water or seriously harming yourself.

MISTAKE #5: NOT ABLE TO understand the cost.

It's true. In the long run living off grid will help you save money. But getting there may require several years. Costs of equipping your home with everything you need to live comfortably and simply could be expensive. You'll certainly save money since you don't have to pay for items like cable and electricity but when you throw in solar panels, garbage disposal products, gardening tools and animals (if you plan to eat outside in your garden) as well as firewood and other costs it's clear how quickly costs increase. Do we not mention the fact that when are not connected to the grid the insurance for your home would rise?

Do not do it Make it a habit to build slowly and then grow the emergency funds.

If you're stuck in the race to get ahead, search for ways to cut costs on your materials and gradually acquire these items. In parallel, you can start making your savings account an emergency fund to cover any unexpected expenses after you've left the grid. There'll be plenty for emergencies, trust us. Develop a plan to earn money even without relying on electricity. Although it's nice to think you'll never have to pay for anything but things do occur. Be sure to have money to cover them.

It's that simple. it. The Five Most Common Off Grid Mistakes and the Ways to Avoid them In the simplest way, you can prepare for self-sufficiency by implementing the practice. To help you get started this checklist:

Make a garden.

Learn to become mechanic.

Find out how you can make own food preserves.

Do your best to live your life frugally.

Learn to care for chickens as well as other farm animals.

Start collecting rainwater today.

Cleanse your drinking water.

Learn to work using wood.

Learn to create an entire kit.

Learn the basics of first aid.

Chapter 3: Composting In An Off Grid Environment

What are off-grid toilets and What is their purpose?

The composting toilet can be your only solution to dispose of waste efficiently and sustainably.

Although boats, RVs THOWS, small-sized houses and off-grinders are among the most frequent customers, these can also be employed by anyone seeking an environmentally sustainable method to dispose of waste.

What's the distinction between composting toilets and regular toilet?

Although many composting toilets are similar to conventional toilets in appearance however, they function in a totally different way.

Toilets that compost, unlike normal toilets, don't make use of water and aren't connected to a septic or sewer system.

This is the reason I love the composting toilet I use.

Toilets that compost are entirely organic and natural, requiring the use of no pipes, chemical or flushing.

What is the procedure for making use of the composting toilet?

Liquids (pee) as well as hard substances (feces) get separated out in the composting toilets (poop)

The return of humus to soil provides the same benefits for ecology similar to adding manure from animal sources from a garden supply store. The liquids are transported into the tank at the front via an opening trapdoor that is fed to the tank below (called the compost area).

This stops the two getting into contact, thus preventing an chemical reaction which creates the smell of sewage (you have probably noticed that smell that can be found inside the toilet for about 30 minutes after the deposit has been left by someone).

The amount of composting you do is determined by the number of times you use the bathroom during the day, the amount of toilet paper you need every time you visit the bathroom and the number of people who reside in your house.

We empty the solids each 3-4 weeks or at least for us. If a composting facility isn't available, you can dump the tank of solids into a composting bag , and dispose of it in the trash (it continues to decompose in the bag and doesn't pose an hazard to the environment). If they're sufficiently far offshore and have enough space, boaters could dump their waste overboard.

The liquids may be dilute and scattered over the ground, dumped into the drain, or dumped into the ocean by boaters (again within a reasonable distance from the shore). For us (2 persons who are full-time users) an average routine for emptying the tank's liquid is once every three days.

The most common concern of people is the smell. The cause is moisture. the smell.

Feces does not smell until it is dried. There is almost no smell through the use of urine diverters to transport fluid away from waste that is solid, and then venting the tank to outside using either a conduit or a fan.

Add an extra scoop from coconut shells, pine shavings or something similar to toilet paper each when you make use of it. It instantly absorbs the water contents and starts decay.

If your bin is overflowing there are several ways to dispose of the garbage. It is possible to put it in a bin and toss it away.

The majority of people living in regions where resources like cities' dumps in short supply will decide to compost their waste in the outside of a bigger barrel.

Human waste has to be fully recycled in a container outside over 18 months prior to when it is returned to the earth as dirt. Poop, just like rain is water that has evaporated and returns in the ground. It took a completely different route.

All things eventually return to the earth, which is among the reasons that drives many people to stay completely off the grid. My motivation comes from the desire to do my part for the environment.

Different types of composting toilets off the Grid

1. Toilets in the Incinolet

They are powered by electricity and require power to warm them, which is a drawback.

They work by evaporating feces before warming it using heat to encourage drying. They should be properly vented and the fecal "chamber is typically ejected out to the outside by an air-flow fan.

The feces will dry to dust and could be tossed into the garbage or left to the soil. It's acceptable to place the feces in a compost pile however, don't apply it to your garden because it might not be secure.

To be considered as sterile, human waste has to be heated to a suitable temperature and for the right period of time.

We'll discuss how to regulate the temperatures as well as timing required for the proper composting of poop in greater details below.

Summary: This kind of composting toilet is perfect for small RV houses, also referred to by the name"THOWS" (tiny house on wheels) however, it is not suitable for people with limited power.

2. The Composting Toilet comes with a Self-Sealing Cartridge Dry Flush

Do you hate everything about toilet sludge and don't want feel, smell or even handle it? It's time to meet your beloved composting toilet... It's so simple to use that you'll be able to forget that you're not connected to your grid...

Press the button when you've finished with your task, and a plastic wraps the trash is sealed, then transfers it to an empty container which can be removed once it's full of sealed bags.

There isn't any smell from this clean toilet. While it requires power, it is feasible attach it the battery of a car for use off-grid. It is possible to run this device with solar power, too.

This one, however it's not all roses and butterflies.

There are many negatives.

To begin you'll have to think about how to dispose of the cartridges, unless you have an established waste collection facility.

In addition, the cost of the bags may increase over time.

If you're as me, then you'll attempt to extend the process by not flushing. This can leave behind a smell even if it's just urine. This seems to be in contradiction with an aspect of the toilet's most beneficial characteristics.

Despite the expense of the bags and the cost of the toilet, it isn't expensive. The average composting toilet is priced at up to $1,500, dry-flush toilets will cost you just a few hundred dollars.

The bottom line is that if you're away from water sources such as running water, and you require self-contained systems that is self-contained, this is an excellent alternative.

What is a composting Toilet and how do I Utilize It?

The compost bins can be self-contained, and typically come with a hand crank on the side to turn into compost.

There are plenty of these available. The 'Nature's Eye' model is one that I would highly recommend. It is available for less than $960 in the event that they are sealed and don't include exhaust fans. The smell is not too bad and the toilet is designed with the look of a typical toilet with a top. It also appears to have a tiny septic tank. The diverter of urine within this tank directs urine flow into bottles located in on the side in the tank.

Once you've completed your task After you've finished, take the bottle outdoors and place it in the woods. Voila your urine is now part of the natural world. If it makes you feel better, men have been doing it for a long time without the aid of the bottle.

It is also important to note that urine contrary to what is commonly believed is not harmful however, it's not sterile.

It's a myth that says sterile urine is a thing.

Your bladder isn't completely sterile and bacteria are discovered in your urine. This is the reality of the science. Don't flush in your garden and then wash your hands afterwards. It's perfectly safe to put it on the soil around the tree's foundation because it's removed from the tree, and then released into the air.

It will then come back to earth as rain. This is how amazing nature can be. The feces are disposed of in larger containers at the rear of the toilet. Don't worry about the goal and it will be exactly where it needs to. The substance breaks down once it is inside the container.

The smell is hidden from your home and emitted to the outside through a vent pipe that is connected to the rear to the tanks. Because there is no urine in the tank The feces will dry out quickly.

A fan with a 12-volt voltage connected to the tank's bottom can aid in speeding drying, however, it's not required. The scent is kept in place by water. Dry poop is more preferable than wet stool.

For the purpose of breaking up the compost, move the knob to the side of the toilet. Before you use the chamber, add coconut fiber or peat moss. The feces will break down faster because of this. The chamber operates similarly to an outside yard waste crank-operated composter.

Around 80 people are able to be placed inside the trash bin. The number of people making use of the facility and the amount of time that passes in a single use for each individual are important elements. After every bathroom use or at least once per day, turn on the light.

This method comes with the additional advantage of allowing you to put your toilet paper into it to break up alongside the remainder of your garbage.

Once the bin is fully filled and covered, put it in an 15-gallon garbage bag, then empty the contents of the bag.

Make sure you take the compost outside, and put it in the compost bin. You can simply throw it into the bin when the garbage bag is compostable.

Before use human compost must be allowed to sit up to 18 months, and must be heated and able to stay hot.

It won't be a problem when you cover your compost in black. Compost produces heat by itself.

You can spread it on the ground at the rear of your home after 18 months.

What is the best composting Toilet

As you will see, there are many possibilities. Here are some ideas:

1. Know the laws of your region.

Toilets that compost aren't permitted in all states, municipalities or counties. Other local regulations like septic require that you be tied to grids, which is why I am bringing you to number 2...

2. Assess whether you require septic tanks.

Prior to making any improvements to your home it is possible that you will need to construct a septic system.

Before investing in the property, make sure that you are aware of the regulations. Septic tanks are an investment that is costly. It is important to take note of that prior making your final decision on the land purchase.

3. Choose the best system that meets your requirements.

The options listed above aren't the only options available since everyone is different, there is no one-size-fits-all solution.

Composting Concepts

There is a good chance that you don't want your compost sitting within an unguarded bin. There is, fortunately there is a solution.

Poop-holding barrels can be purchased sealed and dated for just $20. Be sure to connect an insignificant pipe to the top of the barrel so that moisture can go away and to prevent off-gassing. Keep in mind that we must remove moisture in order to create compost.

Make a small cut inside the barrel's center using an instrument that is placed inside the barrel so that you can keep track of the temperature.

The barrel should be dated at the time it was full. It will remain empty for 18 months from the day it was filled.

Each month, take it out and give it a good stir. This is a safe, way to avoid a mess because it's sealed.

You are able to unload your compost bin following 18 months inside the barrel.

There's plenty of rich black soil within.

You'll require a lot of barrels since you'll be filling more than once in the 18 months.

After the initial one year, you could put the barrels in one big pile and then wrap it in dark plastic, to make sure you keep the barrels warm and dry.

There are many ways to help the compost decomposition process.

Do not be discouraged by the idea of the idea of composting your garbage.

If you're intending to be living off the grid, you'll need to live with it. Also, just to be clear...

You don't have to shell out a lot of money on composting toilets. I repeat that you don't have to shell out a lot of money on composting toilets.

It all boils to how confident you are at completing the task.

Always wear gloves, wash your hands thoroughly and make sure that your containers are tightly sealed and you'll be safe.

Don't be worried. You'll probably be able locate a toilet somewhere.

Chapter 4: Living Off-Grid In A Motorhome

How to live off grid in an RV The Essentials You Need to Be aware of

Although RV living is typically linked to people that have retired, or have saved money to travel, it's important to point out that an overwhelming number of households and individuals have quit their homes and are now reside in off grid RVs. More than 1 million Americans are contemplating living in an RV in the present.

Living the RV lifestyle opens the door to a myriad of possibilities, however, diving deep into living off grid can also bring up a host of concerns. Can you operate the RV like a fully-fledged home? What is the maximum time I can remain in one place and what is the best place to go?

What should I look out for when buying an RV?

I've conducted a lot of study on the subject of living off road in an RV. While there are plenty of concerns, there are many solutions. Let's look at each in turn.

Before purchasing an RV There are some aspects to take into consideration.

Is the open road calling you to embark for a trip? If the answer is yes, then an RV might be the ideal option to go off-grid camping. It is important to recognize that, there are so many options out there, buying an RV could be a challenge.

In the end, determining the quality of an RV is worthy to buy on first sight isn't easy. Before you make a purchase there are some factors to take into consideration when buying an RV.

1. What will you do with It?

The first thing you need to think about when buying an RV is whether you plan to only use it to go camping or live off grid. A camping trip could be between one and two weeks. It's also crucial to take into consideration how many items you'll need to pack and also who will be travelling with you. This is an excellent way to determine which size RV will work best for your group as well as your budget.

2. Check for maintenance records.

Without doubt the most important aspect to take into consideration when buying an RV is its maintenance documents. Anyone who is satisfied by the quality of the vehicle will be happy to provide you with the vehicle's maintenance documents. You can be sure that your RV won't cause issues if you choose to go camping off grid with your family simply by reviewing its maintenance records.

While reviewing the documents be sure to look for any consistency in the oil changes to discern if they've been changed regularly and you should follow the recommendations of the manufacturer. Apart from reviewing the intervals for oil changes and intervals, it's also an excellent idea to check whether the timing belt is adjusted, particularly if the vehicle is near or over the 60,000 mile mark.

3. Check the area for signs of leaks or odors.

If you're considering purchasing a used motorhome, then this will be extremely crucial. Be sure to check that every part on the RV is working in condition and there aren't any issues that could compromise the camping experience off grid. Before you purchase I would strongly suggest to check the vehicle for smells as well as leaks, molds and awnings, as well as the roof.

It would be beneficial if you had someone with you to make sure that nothing is missed in the inspection. Bring flashlights to help you inspect the rig as well as the areas that are dark inside the RV.

If you're working on a tight budget, picking RVs with some flaws will help you save cash (depending on the price of repairs, obviously). If you think that there are too many issues and the cost is too expensive, you can negotiate against the vendor to ensure you can save cash in the process.

4. Check the tires

It's essential to examine tire wear and tear especially if you're planning to purchase an RV that is used. Whatever the tire's condition or condition, it's advised to replace it every 6 years. If you own a luxury vehicle and tires are expensive and replacing them could take an arm leg.

Utilizing your hands to spot flaws or cracks is among the most effective ways to test the quality of the tire. In addition to inspecting the tires on your vehicle It's also an excellent idea to examine on the tire that is spare to confirm that all the tires are the same model and type.

Another way to gauge the quality of a tire is to check the age of the tire. It is easy to determine the age of a tire by looking at the numbers and letters inscribed on the sides. The most frequent markings for tires comprise the letters "US DOT" as well as a four-digit number which indicates the year of manufacture.

5. Request an Test Drive

You've double-checked the components and everything seems to be in good order. The only thing to be accomplished first, and that's to inquire about a test drive with the seller. Test drives give you an idea of the way the RV rides in the road and the level of performance you will be able to achieve driving it. This could be a decisive element in deciding whether you'd like to stay in an RV for the duration of your life.

You can drive the RV on free highways (especially when this is your first experience taking it for a drive) to see how it responds to different speeds as well as brakes and turns. If the RV is moving be aware of any objects that bounce or are shaking. It is vital to note that the vehicle you test drive is small in size and will increase in weight when you fill it up with personal items.

Naturally, you're not required to purchase an RV today. Maybe you'd like to find out whether the idea of living with an RV the right choice for you before making a decision. Perhaps you'd like to examine the specific model of an RV before buying it. In this case, go to RVshare and reserve an RV. The site offers a wide range of recreational vehicles can be rented directly by local owner.

Specifics of an RV that are important

The practicality of the RV and the cozy atmosphere the RV creates are two things to think about when purchasing an RV. Here are some of the features that should be part of every RV.

1. Storage Tanks for Water Storage Tanks

A RV's tank for water is typically measured by the length of it. It is essential to select an RV with water tanks that are easily connected to water systems. In this way, particularly when you reside in off-grid trailers, you will get a steady supply of fresh water.

Cleansing and disinfecting water tanks is a vital aspect to maintaining the water system of your RV. To prevent illness and serious illnesses, ensure that the black or wastewater is delivered through pipes that are located on other side than the drinking water system.

A.A 16 Gallon Fresh/Gray RV Water Tank is a product I'd suggest for an vehicle (on Amazon). It's a reliable 16-gallon tank that is made from FDA-approved and robust polyethylene. Since this tank is constructed completely of only one piece of material, you won't need to worry about breaking in the seams. It is easy to put together and is resistant to corrosion as well as rust, staining and stains. An excellent alternative as a mobile residence!

2. Restroom

One of the major advantages of travel by RV is the accessibility to bathroom facilities. Most off-grid trailers have a decent bathroom, with toilet, shower, and seating. Although they do not require a lot of space small RV bathrooms are typically crowded into cramped space, causing everything in the bathroom to become wet.

Large RVs are advised for bathrooms with adequate size since they come with a small tub or stand-up shower and an additional sink and toilet.

If you're looking to wash your clothing, you'll need a wash machine that is portable can be sufficient.

3. Electricity use

A typical camper didn't have electricity at one point in time. I'm not certain that such an arrangement will work for everyone today. A majority of RVs currently have some sort of electric power. Consider a large DC battery. Since many campgrounds offer AC power through hookups, RV builders have installed AC/DC converters that allow the battery to be charged even while within.

But, if your vehicle includes a large amount of devices, a 12-volt battery may not be sufficient. A lot of RVs come with a generator built-in. It allows people to travel for a longer period of time and become independent in terms of electrical power. It is the power source for your television, refrigerator and computer. It also powers your toaster, computer and even your coffee maker. It's your personal powerhouse!

Generators require the usage of fuel, which can be propane or diesel or gasoline. This means that you'll need to replenish the gasoline containers on a regular basis.

For a boost to your power supply it is recommended to purchase an small solar system that can be carried around.

4. Slide-Out Displays

Slide-outs are among the most appealing features in an RV. In most instances, will help increase the dimensions of an RV, making it appear bigger than it actually is. But, keep in mind that slides can substantially add weight to your set-up, so be sure to ensure that you have enough space to slide out.

A slide-out system requires periodic maintenance. It is recommended that the seals are washed at least twice a year with a conditioner in order to ensure they are in good shape.

5. Kitchen

Off-road trailers also have kitchens, which typically include refrigerators, a high-quality sink, as well as a range of cooking equipment. A good RV kitchen also has an area to keep your food items cutting boards, mugs, cutting boards Tupperware containers as well as coffee pots and pans as well as other essentials for cooking.

Refrigerators in modern RVs are typically powered by electricity as well as gas. If you're looking to include a microwave in your home kitchen, then may also add a small generator.

6. RV Safety

If you are leaving your RV to go on a hike or to sleep the RV must be secured. Don't leave valuables or your family members alone. RVLock Key Fob and RH Compact Keyless Entry Keypad are both highly rated products available on Amazon. It secures your entrance door and can be used with almost any automobile that is a recreational vehicle. It only takes some minutes to install and will ensure your safety throughout your trip. Keyless handles Keypad with more than 1 million codes possible and an accessory fob for remotes (up to 10) keys that are mechanical, and four AAA batteries are all included. An ideal solution that guarantees the security and safety of your RV throughout the day.

7. Storage in the basement

A gorgeous basement storage space is another feature of a fantastic RV, where you can store your furniture, carpets outdoor tables, other bicycles, and other accessories. Comparatively to other kinds of off-road trailers the Class A RVs have a bigger basement, and considerably more storage space. There are some class C RVs with enough room for your other needs as well.

8. Floor coverings

The flooring in your RV should be flexible to your needs and preferences. This is a cost-effective method to provide your RV with a elegant, new-look. Most of the time, replacing and removing the flooring of your carpet can be completed in just a couple of minutes on your own.

9. Sleeping Accommodations

It should be obvious. Beds are essential in any mobile residence. Beds are the primary element that turns any wall into a space that is suitable to human beings every time people think of their home, or perhaps the hotel room.

If you're on a spending plan, the bed may be inadequate. This is especially relevant for family members. The most important thing you require is a bedroom. an individual space inside the RV, separated from the remainder of the living space. Two or more bedrooms are standard in family-oriented RVs, providing room for parents and children.

I would suggest purchasing an RV that has an all-weather bed. This is an essential feature unless you are looking to cut costs and buy an extremely small RV. If it's a double bed the two partners will each be able to access their bed from a different angle and will not have to cross over the other's bed. This makes the process of creating the bed much simpler.

If you wish for your bedroom to be a secret from your children the bedroom should be entered through a door, not curtains. In order to make the car lighter, some sellers of RVs change the doors to curtains. I do not believe that you have to put your privacy risk.

10. Seating and dining Area

This is a different important aspect of a RV arrangement that is largely contingent on how many persons travelling together. There are also visitors who may visit at times. For meals and entertainment everyone in the family and guest should have a seat. Take into consideration these factors before deciding on the dimensions number, configuration, and quantity of seating areas. Be sure to ensure that your seats face the entertainment center correctly in the event that you are adding the TV or game system.

How to Begin in an off-grid RV

1. Find a location that is suitable

The location is the first goal. The advantages of having being in an RV is the fact that it permits you to roam around without restriction. It is always possible to find parking spots or a place to camp in for a night, or two prior to heading off towards your next destination. There are public land areas in the United States where you can stay at no cost, but I think they're limited by 14 days. In my essay about a self-contained RV I spoke of free parking spots. It's also possible of purchasing the property and parking your vehicle there forever.

Once you've determined where you'll place your car, conduct some research into the weather conditions in the region. What's the weather like at night there? In an RV, sleeping outside on a hot, cold or humid day could be a problem. Also, modern RVs are equipped with superior wall separation and heating, air conditioning as well as other facilities. But, think about the climate of the area is in line with your personal preferences. Not everyone is a fan of and accepts every kind of weather.

Find out where important close-by facilities are. It is necessary to locate all the required structures, like markets and medical facilities. In addition, if you're not looking to spend for the whole day in your RV, but want to relax from exploring the natural world take a look at the entertainment options in your area, including movie and conventional restaurants, theaters, amusement parks, and so on.

2. Get Your RV Set

Examine thoroughly your RV when you are preparing for a life off the grid. Decide on the tools and equipment it'll require prior to hitting the road. Plates, tools, tools to repair, electrical appliances, and more. Are there carpets in your home? If so, you'll need to purchase an air cleaner. Do you have flooring composed from wood? Bring the Broom. Make a list of all the groceries and don't leave your home until you've crossed all of your items off.

Make sure to check out the RV's facilities and amenities. Does it make sense to refill the tank of water with new water? Perhaps chlorine is required to further filter the water. Are the septic tanks empty? If not, you should stop at a waste disposal facility while you are on the way out. Inspect the propane tanks, and, if needed refill them. Also the batteries of all RVs are required to be recharged.

It's time to go when you've finished all this.

3. Plan your actions and stick to it.

After you've reached the spot you've chosen, test to explore a variety of parking options to maximize the sun and shade. Build a pad for your RV to rest on if you're planning to make it your permanent place of residence. If you're in the vicinity and are interested in the area, try to make new acquaintances who could be able provide you with plenty of information on the area.

Establish routines that will maintain your RV and its facilities in good condition. Make sure to check the oil, tires gasoline, and other necessities regularly the same way you do in a normal automobile. Create a schedule and adhere to it: drain the drain, fill up tanks for propane and water and make sure you buy your groceries regularly.

If you are planning to go away after a few days be sure that the property is clean and tidy. We don't want negative effects on the natural ecosystem. You'll be on the road to freedom if you follow the steps 1 , 2 and 3.

Is it possible to live off The Grid with an RV?

This is a topic that deserves a lot of thought. Let's suppose you've found that perfect RV, purchased all the essential equipment and tools and are now in the process of launching your journey. You can park wherever you want and enjoy a rent-free living off-grid. Are you able to be completely off grid?

The simple answer is that it's feasible with a high-end modern, modern RV. There are other steps to take.

Of course, all RVs are suitable for camping on dry land. This means that you don't have to depend on the availability of hookups when traveling. Boondocking is a different name for this. Like we said the typical RV comes with water tanks and a waste tank, and possibly batteries or a generator. They aren't the ideal choice for those who want to stay off the grid for a long period of time. Therefore, it's time to make the switch.

Many RVs, such as come with an excellent generator that can produce electricity without needing any power source. But, you'll need gasoline to power it. I would suggest installing some solar panels on the outside of your motorhome to boost your power source.

Solar panels utilize the sun's energy to create electricity that is clean and long-lasting method of power that doesn't emit harmful gasses or make you travel to town to purchase more propane. Another dependence strand is cut off and you're a steps closer to being without electricity.

It is important to keep in mind that contact with the world is necessary. It is necessary to go to an area town frequently to buy fresh food or refill your water tank and clean out the trash tank eliminate garbage, change broken parts or tools for example. But if you conserve water and make an exhaustive shopping list, you could remain in the wilderness for longer. If you are careful with your budget and carefully, the expense of living off grid could be reduced.

I've also discussed the issue that climate changes are a factor. If you'd like to be able to spend more time away from the city ensure that your RV is capable of handling the four seasons. If it is able to be able to withstand weather fluctuations and a vehicle with adequate insulation could help you avoid a lot of hassle. Additionally, as you experience a change in seasons, you should consider going out, at least to places where conditions are nice. You'll save money which would otherwise be used to operate the heater and air conditioner.

The ultimate off-grid experience is possible by taking these additional precautions and taking care regarding your RV's maintenance and equipment. The only thing I'm asking is that you not damage or harm your surroundings. Don't ignite the forest fire, do not litter, and work to minimize the environmental impact of your activities to the greatest extent possible. It's what it's like"being "off from the power grid."

The Top Recreational Vehicles on the Market

1. Airstream Classic

Airstream Classic Airstream Classic is among the most well-known RVs available today it was designed by the well-known US manufacturer of trailers Airstream. The first off-road car, introduced in 1936, comes with the designated bedroom, lounging kitchen, dining and lounging areas and is between 30 and 33 feet in length.

It also has intelligent control technology that lets you control the most important aspects of your vehicle regardless of where you are. Airstream Classic is available for purchase now. Airstream Classic now has a beginning price of $152,400.

2. Thor Quantum LF31

If you're looking for a cheaper alternatives to Airstream Classic, the Thor Quantum LF31 is an excellent option. The motor home in class C is priced at more than $132,000, includes an oversized queen-sized bed, two air conditioners, dual televisions as well as a high-quality refrigerator. The chassis is one of the Ford E-450 Super Duty with the capacity of 420 lb-ft and an 6.8 Liter Triton V-10.

3. 2020 Newell Coach P50

Its 2020 Newell Coach P50 is an upgrade from the model of 2019 that comes with six LED floor lamps as well as the power of four window blinds with two patio awnings, two sliding storage beds an in-built camera system with a multi-function remote and window frames that flush, as well as other features. The interior is also gorgeous, with a front lounge with a deluxe leather co-pilot and pilot chairs which adjust in six ways.

A bedroom, galley bathroom with a large size as well as outdoor and indoor entertainment equipment garbage disposals, intrepid monitors and the ability to monitor tire pressure complete the features of the P50. The P50 costs $2,107,450 and is available only within Miami and the states of Oklahoma as well as Miami.

4. KZ-RV Sportsmen S330IK

A triple slide on the KZ-RV Sportsmen S330IK makes for a nice interior composition, and also a pleasing bedroom configuration. Different caps for freshwater, wastewater gray water, LP gas and water heaters are included in this trailer off the road.

It's renowned for its top-of-the-line design and construction and its light and feathery towing. Blinded windows, auto-adjustable brakes with electric motors and radial tires, a queen-sized mattresses, an upholstered headboard and an LCD monitor are just a few of other amenities that come with this Sportsmen model. This model will set you at around $28,705.

5. Jay Flight 28BHBE

Jay Flight 29BHBE Jay Flight 29BHBE designed by Jayco and comes with incredible features that include a sturdy slide-out, which extends the living and kitchen areas. The model also comes with Sway Command Control Technology, which is essential to ensure that your tires don't get out of control when you take to the road.

Jay Flight 28BHBE Jay Flight 28BHBE model is the latest version of the series it has an in-shower shower, a pass-through storage area and double bunk beds. It also has an enormous U-dinette and folding outs. In addition the freshwater tanks can hold 38 gallons of water as the black and gray tanks can contain 39 gallons of wastewater. It is priced at around $24,995.

6. Forrest River Rockwood Tent Camper Trailers

Here's something more affordable. The trailers made by this company are lightweight and small and cost between $10,000 and $20,000. They can be towable using an auto, so they come with an excellent folding trailer to carry wherever you want to. When you take the trailer away there's plenty of space and amenities such as a dining space with a shower, a kitchen and two comfy beds. If your trailer folds back you'll have a trailer just under 6 feet high and is easy to pull. Because a lighter trailer places less strain on your vehicle, you'll be able to save cash on fuel. It's true that this isn't an actual RV but it's a decent alternative.

7. Winnebago Intent

Think about getting your RVing adventure begun by purchasing the Winnebago motorhome. The price of this Class A motorhome is approximately $116,000. It comes with all the basics features, and certain extras. Great visibility on the road with plenty of storage space excellent lounge and dining areas, as well as the option of four different floor plans to pick from. You can also get an awning for the patio that is motorized.

8. Thor Chateau

Thor Motor Coach's Chateau Motorhome is a fantastic Alternative to Class C. It's possibly the most flexible of the options on this list, having 13 different floor plans ranging between 24 and 32 feet of space to choose from. If you're a buyer you're in total control in deciding which one best suits your needs. Beautiful kitchens, bathrooms and enough bedrooms to accommodate a family of four are all part of the plans. The most spacious layout has enough space for seven people! $91,200 to $120,750 is the price range.

9. Unity by Leisure Travel Vans

This class-leading beauty will let you feel at ease in the car. Despite its size, this model is highly aerodynamic and comes with massive frameless windows that provide an unobstructed view. Six-floor designs are offered to any off-gridder or traveler to select from. The various types of beds (murphy corner, corner, island and twin bed) come in various Unity designs along with huge entertainment spaces. With lots of storage space as well as the possibility of having two different living spaces, the utilization of space is both unique and amazing. The base price is $134,210.

10. Winnebago Vista

Its Vista range, a different offering by Winnebago Industries, is a leap forward in the realm of motorhomes for families. It is packed with useful and stylish features that can transform the vehicle into a real home with the comfortable LED lighting and an electric patio awning and a front shade, a stunning dining area and a fully-equipped kitchen, and so much more. It even has a fireplace! There are four flooring designs available and each comes with the double slideout. Prices start at $138,000 and rises from the point.

If you're interested in learning more about the various kinds of RVs I suggest you check out my article on self-contained RVs as well as their classifications.

Always double-check everything

The condition of the RV

Features

Brand endorsements

Inspect the RV's system to determine if they require to be replenished.

Locations in which you intend to stay

What you decide to do each day is entirely your choice.

The most important thing is to take your time and have fun. Take pleasure in the journey, the excitement, and the feeling of being free. The world is open before your eyes, and you've got an RV that is reliable to get you where you need to travel.

Chapter 5: Methods Of Preserving Food

For many off-gridders, preparing and hunting food is an most enjoyable aspect, however, the storage of food for later use is the most difficult part. Nature has a pattern that says food is abundant at certain seasons and those who wish to be independent and free from the industrial food system must be able to manage their food items to ensure that they are ready for consumption throughout the year.

What can I do to keep food in storage if I'm not connected with the internet? To preserve their food items, our forefathers employed a variety of strategies that included:

Smoking, Salting or Drying or Canning

* Vinegar Root Cellar Dry Storage Pickling / Fermentation / Vinegar Root Cellar

* Ice box

* Suet/Fat Storage Chest Freezer with Off-Grid Power

*Slaked Lime Honey or Wood Ashes

Follow me as I discuss the advantages of these low-cost and off-grid food storage strategies.

The Essentials of Food Storage Off-Grid

The storage of food involves the process of making sure that the food you have worked so hard to cultivate and collect doesn't spoil and is available for months at an time. A combination of the following conditions could hinder or delay the growth of bacteria, fungi and molds that hinder preservation:

The problem is that it's hot, or too cold.

* Too acidic/acidic/acidic/acidic/acidic/a
* Too salty or too sweet
* It's dry.

Other than naturally long-lasting crops like squash and some varieties of apples, every conventional food storage technique takes advantage of some or all of the above situations to store harvests to be used later for consumption.

Canning Food for Storage off the Grid

When it comes to the storage of food items for the long-term in the long run, canned food is usually the first thought that is thought of. The following steps are required for this process:

Jars with lids made from glass

- A pressure cooker or canner
* A high-quality canning table book, similar to the well-known "Blue Book" that is no longer blue.

Traditional lids for metal canning jars are, unfortunately, considered an item that is only used once and should be replaced annually. However, there are "indefinitely reuseable" canning lids that are reusable.

Canning works on the idea of sealing cooked fruit vegetables, meats jams, soups, and even milk, in an airtight container. The container is then cooked enough time to get rid of any bacteria that might harm the contents.

Botulism is a rare condition that is caused by Clostridium botulinum, and its related bacteria is the greatest security risk for home preservation of food items. The bacteria thrive in low oxygen areas, such as the insides of jars for canning however they are not able to take sugar, acid or salt. This means that certain things, like jam and salsa, are able to be safely canned with only boiling water. Most meats, vegetables and soups, on other hand, have to be sterilized using an pressure cooker at higher temperatures to make sure they are safe.

Follow the guidelines of a reliable source for making cans, like canning with the Ball Blue Book. Many state universities across the United States have an extension service that gives no-cost information about canning as well as pressure cooker tests.

Smoking, drying and salting

Smoking, salting and drying are the most common methods to cook meat, but they can also be utilized to cook a variety fruit and vegetable.

The purpose behind these strategies is to lower the moisture content of food to a degree that it will not get spoiled. In addition smoking and salting food can cause the presence of salt or acid within the diet, which hinders the growth of your child. Pickling is, however is not salty, but it's wet (more information below).

Most of the time salting requires an airy, dry space where the meat can cure. This can be within one of the roofs in building or barn, in a specific room, or an entirely separate structure designed specifically for this specific purpose.

Smoking requires an use of smoker or smoker for the application of the smoke. Smoking meat is done by smoke that is hot and cold. Smoking in hot temperatures can also heat the meat and is not typically used for storage. Today cold smoking, not only is used to soak raw meat in cold smoke, but it's often "cured" by using preservatives. Preservatives were not employed before.

Since salt removes moisture, and the smoke is already dry The smoking and salting process helps in drying process of the meat. The direct application of low heat to the fruits and vegetables helps in the drying process. Here are a few ways to do this:

* It's simply a table in the sunlight.
* Low-temperature solar dehydrator
* Tomato Paste made from Sun-Dried Tomatoes

Pickling and Fermentation

The competition that occurs between "good" bacteria in fermentation and pickling techniques can be used to eliminate harmful bacteria. Fermented foods comprise the following:

Sauerkraut

Kimchi

Kombucha

Miso

Pickles

Cheese

Vinegar

Wine and beer

Traditional fermentation is a method to ferment virtually every vegetable. This is known as "Lacto-fermentation," but it's essentially the same as sauerkraut and pickles.

Vegetable Fermentation Techniques

Add 1-3 tablespoons for each one quart of water to create brine.

Fill the jar to about halfway full of vegetables, then cover it with brine.

Allow for a period of 1-2 weeks at a cooler, out of the sun place.

Sauerkraut

Sauerkraut is like the previous one, with the exception that it is spiced with salt directly to the cabbage grated at a rate of one tablespoon for every 1.75 pounds of vegetables. After adding salt crushing the cabbage by hand (or feet as it is traditionally). After about 15 minutes, the cabbage will release enough water to completely cover the packed cabbage. However, if you need to, add a small amount of brine to make sure that all the krauts are fully covered.

Onion and Garlic Vegetables to Dry Storage

Dry Storage and Root Cellars

Certain food items can be stored in a cold, damp area referred to as a root cellar as many roots vegetables are kept in it. They could be as simple as a hole dug in the ground in front of the house or underneath it. The following food items will work well in a root cellar

* Apples
* Beets
* Broccoli
* Brussels Sprouts
* Cabbage
* Carrots
* Artichokes
* Leaks

* Parsnips
* Pears
* Potatoes
* Rutabagas
* Turnips
* Radishes

The phrase "dry storage" is a reference to a cool dry space or pantry. Dry storage is great for:

* Any kind of dried beans
* Pumpkins
* Squash
* Sweet potatoes
* Garlic Onions
* Grains
* Tomatoes

Simple Off-Grid Refrigeration - the Cold Box

The most common method for storing food is the refrigerator. In a well-developed county most people would feel uncomfortable in a house without any kind of refrigeration.

There were many low-tech alternatives to electricity before it became widespread. The most basic one was an adequately insulated "cold box" with a tiny access point to the home's shaded side. In summer, this allowed an access point to coldest temperatures and was a decent storage area for perishable items. Of course, the colder temperature can help preserve food in winter months, but the cold box can be used to store things that are cooler than your kitchen, but not so cold that they would freeze.

Ice Box at a low Cost

The icebox is a leap ahead in terms of ease and sophistication. Iceboxes have been in use for centuries , and are insulated boxes that have a compartment to store blocks of ice. It is basically a longer-lasting cooler. Before the advent of electric energy, it was sourced from an icehouse, in which winter ice was stored and stored throughout the through the year. The ice was typically taken from nearby lakes in areas of cold weather, but it was also brought to the north in warmer climates.

A modern ice home can be constructed at the cost of an easily insulated shed. In the northern part of the country modern homesteader can easily freeze huge cubes of ice outside in the winter months and then put them away for use in the summer. Because they melt less quickly bigger blocks, as big as you are able to handle and store for the longest time.

Refrigeration Off Grid

Off-Grid Chest Freezer for the Lowest Cost

Modern refrigerators and freezers are feasible when you are off grid using off-grid energy solutions.

If you're using off-grid solar it is possible to have a cheap chest freezer, or even two may be a viable option. Chest freezers are especially efficient and a skilled homesteader could increase the capacity by adding insulation. Additionally, they are compatible with off-grid solar because freezers consume more power in the summer when sun shines, which is the time when solar panels are able to produce more power.

It is possible to use an additional chest freezer to make an off-grid refrigerator with high efficiency. You can turn your cheap Craigslist chest freezer into a very efficient refrigerator with perfect temperature control with a simple thermometer-controlled outlet like this.

Other techniques that are based on time

Food items can be stored in many ways, like coating them with non-rancid fats like Lard or frying them, covering them with an ash layer, candying them with honey, or submerging the food items in lime slaked (a product made from seashells and limestone).

A Note on Preservatives within the 21st Century

If you've read food labels over the last fifty years, you've probably seen a range of potentially hazardous food chemicals and preservatives. Modern preservatives destroy microorganisms that cause the food to spoil and can cause poisons that isn't strong enough to inflict harm on those that consume them.

These are some of the examples of the current preservatives available:

* Sodium Benzoate
* Sodium Nitrate and Nitrite (aka "curing salt")
* Sulfur Dioxide

* Propyl Paraben
* BHA and BHT (aka butylated hydroxyanisole, and butylated hydroxytoluene)
* Since modern preservatives are part of industrial chemistry and are not readily available at home I won't go over the subject in depth here.

The most important thing to bear on your mind is the fact that sodium Nitrate/Nitrite is a well-known substitute for potassium sodium nitrate (saltpeter) which is essential to enhance the texture and taste of meats that have been cured. Making saltpeter out of urine and ashes has been previously done and could make a natural preservative that is suitable for homesteaders. However, I'm not going explore it now.

Chapter 6 Security And Protection Off-Grid

Living away from the grid gives you a sense of freedom, it has its own responsibility. It is possible to be held responsible for all the responsibilities you have for yourself, even in the event that municipal governments don't provide services common to all communities. Although this may not seem like a big problem for many of these services, there's one that stands out above other services and that is security.

Since your home off grid is probably outside of the majority of jurisdictions and is likely far enough from where the local authority's headquarters are located to be able to contact you promptly if you require assistance It is essential to consider how you can ensure the security of your property. There are many options you can choose from, dependent on your preferences and available resources. This is why we've created seven ways to ensure your home is secure and secure:

1. Alarms are used to alert people.

The technology may employ the power generated by green methods (such as solar or wind arrays) or in analog ways. Whatever method you choose to use getting an early warning in the event of trespassers entering your property is recommended, particularly in the case of living away from the grid and are probably out of the local law enforcement authority.

If you're looking for a low-tech method using cans as wire trick is the most basic and most effective methods. In this instance you'll tie up a few cans close enough together that they will rattle when the cans are jostled. There's no need for a lengthy line of cans that is at an angle, which is not the case in films or other media portrayals. Although this might catch some people off-guard, it's nonetheless too visible to effectively serve. Instead, put the strung-up cans in a ring behind plants or at the wire's tie-off points. Even if they cross the wire, there'll be plenty of sound.

Current content from the Off Grid World

The main drawback of this method is that it can cause false alarms during windy conditions and is only effective for a short on the area. It's an ideal choice to install an alarm system that is electronic if you are able to generate your own electric power. Be aware that the alarm is not likely to communicate with the third party , but will instead issue an alarm sound when someone comes close. However, wild animals could trigger the alarm that will be heard for miles. But, the risk decreases with time as wildlife around the region discovers what triggers and does not trigger the alarm by trial and trial and.

2. Lamps

This security gadget is similar to the alarm that responds however it's visual instead of aural and is operated by electric power. If you aren't able to produce electricity using the wind or sun the lights are likely to be an option if your plans are to invest a substantial amount of cash on deep-cycle battery. Although you probably have batteries that can be used for a variety of applications, this expense isn't on your list of priorities.

In terms of lighting you have two choices: Always on or sometimes. Utilizing a number of high-powered floodlights to keep the space around your home illuminated at night can be easiest to set up. It also has the benefit of not going out of service until the electrical system in its entirety is destroyed. The main drawback is that although light can dissuade trespassers from entering your property, it can also provide the trespassers with information regarding the location of your home. It is possible to install lighting that only turns on at the moment they are activated.

It is the most efficient, practical and safe method to ensure your home is protected by lighting. But, since it is based on the addition of new components to complete the system, it is more prone to failure but this isn't likely when you choose high-quality components and test them thoroughly before installing it. In essence, the lights that trigger should be the same floodlights are typically used however these lights activate under the influence of motion detection. The issue arises because wild animals can be prone to trigger the lights, however this time, they're unlikely to connect it with their activities, and they are most likely to trigger it.

3. Canines

Since the time we brought them under control Man's favorite pet is used to defend properties and the people. Dog breeds of all kinds are eager to help by protecting their home and their family members at a cost of feeding them and giving them a cozy shelter. If you select the right breed, you might not require any additional instruction or direction. Dogs' instincts will prevail, and the best methods of defense will be revealed.

There are several aspects to consider when you are buying a dog to help with defense. The most important thing to bear in mind is that choosing an animal with the ability to do anything that aids in defense isn't always easy. So it is essential to select a breed with care or choose one that has the ability to be trained to offer more effective protection methods. The instincts to protect and alert are the two primary qualities to be looking for.

The majority of breeds possess acute instincts, though some are more naturally developed than others. For instance dogs that have not been designed to give advance warnings of real danger could bark each when it observes the squirrel running into the tree. However guard dogs' behaviors could differ depending on whether they're protecting an area or "pack"-of which humans are typically thought to be.

You'll need a dog that naturally enjoys both of these tasks and also smart enough to know when they are truly required. Shepherd dogs are usually the best option for this but you'll need to learn about their routines and behavior if you live away from the grid. Since many shepherd dogs have a tendency to roam the boundaries of their property and are often far from their homes to fulfill their purpose.

4. Obstacles

The best way to stop any trespasser from being danger towards you would be to make it difficult for them to come near you to begin with. The ideal way to achieve this task may be to create several forms of difficult-to-overcome barriers. Barriers that are extended and local are a good method, but you'll prefer employing both instead of one or the other.

In this instance the extended barrier will serve as the first defensive line. This can be that is as simple as fencing. Of of course, if you have large areas of land, building the chain link or timber fence is not feasible. The cost is greater than the benefits of the fence. In addition, these types of fences do not work in keeping out people.

For the alternative, either barbed wire or an electronic fence is sufficient. Although a fence made of barbed wire may electrify but this could pose a danger of abuse by animals. It is because wild animals are likely to get caught in a barbed wire fencing at one point and when the fence is electric the animals will fight until exhaustion occurs or pass out from stress.

Concerning local obstacles to stop an intrusion into your home in the first place usually requires an effective set of locks, and perhaps strengthening the windows. If you are considering locks, make sure that they are reinforced with bars that extend beyond the floor, and possibly the ceiling, to stop an intruder from simply smashing them. The only option that is truly secure with regard to windows would be to set up bars, which is not the best option to go down.

5. Environment

The use of the earth to help increase security is possibly the most ancient form of defense that people have used since the beginning of agriculture and the growth of communities. It is important to identify several obstacles along with certain advantages that you can enjoy in this respect.

Being aware of where danger is, for instance is one of the most essential aspects to take care of it. In the end having an unobstructed line of sight in the vicinity of your home is crucial. For those who live within woods, it's an excellent idea to clear a big enough area to detect a danger prior to it getting close to your home.

However the location of an off-grid house could provide some protection from the elements. There's a reason that it's essential to build your home on hills and maintain the higher ground. In the first place, it provides the homeowner a greater view over a house that is situated on the ground. Also, going uphill requires considerably more energy than travelling downhill, which makes any risk more exhausted than it otherwise be. If the danger is a person who has firearms, shooting accurately up the hill is harder than shooting in a straight terrain or down.

The issue of properly securing windows in the way you want them to is, as we've said in the previous paragraph, is the last element of using landscapes to protect yourself. Instead of putting bars on windows, you could use the elevation of your home to render using windows as a entry point impossible. The steps on porches are able to transfer the danger to doors, which need to be secured and strengthened.

6. Traps

If deterrence is not successful and a trespasser has the intention to become an intruder to the property you live on, then you'll be required to take more drastic measures. It is preferred to handle the trespasser in an indirect manner, since this places you in the least level of risk. There are many traps that are able to disarm an intruder or severely hurt them, based on your determination to do harm to the trespasser.

Snares can be a useful way to stop the trespasser from moving further. You can set up several snares in your yard with sturdy, solid steel wire, making it difficult for trespassers to escape should they be taken prisoner. They can additionally be utilized to capture small game and provide another source of food for.

There are a myriad of traps that may cause moderate to severe injuries based upon the dimensions of your house and if you're more worried about the physical health of a burglar who is extremely driven. An easy foot-trap could stop trespassers from moving but without causing more harm than a quick attack at their foot or calf. Bear traps can also be used to deter anyone or any thing trapped in their traps from moving further. Remember that you need to check the local regulations to see whether traps are allowed on your property. In addition, you'll most likely have to issue warnings in the event that they are allowed otherwise you are at risk of legal liability even if another violates the laws.

7. Weapons

Most of the defenses we've examined to date rely on deterrence or indirect methods of protection to offer security. The best way to deal with the trespasser is to stop them from doing so at some point in the future or even at all it is possible that someone will ignore the warning signs that you have put up to remind them that trespassing onto your property is not a good idea.

It is possible that you will have to make things the hands of your personal instance. Utilizing your hands and any similar close-quarters battle method is, however is not a good idea since it can put you at risk. In the event of you are living in a remote area gun ownership is the most secure method of security, at the very the very least. There's a good likelihood that you have an arsenal due to a variety of reasons.

If you hunt in the area near your house the gun you take could be utilized as a security precaution should things go out of hands. But the gun of interest is important in regards to when and how it can be employed. For instance, a rifle is a great weapon for shooting large wildlife from a distance however, it's not likely in its effectiveness if an intruder is less than 10 miles. In this situation shooting with a shotgun is the preferred weapon.

Remember that using firearms does not need to be a death sentence. Farmers and those who live outside of the confines of dense, large societies have used rock salt to replace deadly ammunition for more than 100 years. Although it's effective in killing, odds of that happening are very low. In fact, you're much most likely to leave your attacker with a scalding wound that allows the attacker to escape quickly.

How to Live Legally Off Grid

People who are thinking of living off grid are often scared they'll break the law by doing it. Although going against the grain and living off grid are becoming increasingly and more popular but it can be a bit daunting initially. It is best to be comfortable with some common-sense strategies and a basic understanding however.

How can you live off the grid in a legal manner within the United States. Within the United States, it is legal to live off grid. But, there is several local laws, state, and county rules that govern certain aspects of what you can and cannot do on your property.

When it comes to getting off the grid legally one of the main things you need to be aware of is to conduct your research and find out the specific restrictions that apply to your particular situation. The vast maze of regulations that construction companies and utilities, developers and farmers regularly negotiate isn't easy to find a simple way to navigate because living off grid isn't yet commonplace. Being off grid, as opposed to living a standard life, requires some effort and a little imagination from your side. It's not necessary to tackle it on your own However, it is a challenge. I'll cover some of the most important things you should learn to live free of the grid within America. United States in the sections below.

The Legality of Going Off the Grid

It is possible to live and flourish for a lengthy period of time by not observing the law and residing in the proper areas however, the threat of the authorities can be a bit unsettling. The goal of our lives is to lead an independent life, recognizing and adhering to the rules of your region. This could require some ingenuity from your side or may be a matter of following the law according in full, however nothing more.

The most difficult part of living off the grid and complying with the rules is that they are manyof them, and they come from many directions. There is no one law or set of laws you have to follow. It is a fact that nobody can be sure that they're following all regulations that apply, regardless of regardless of whether they live in a remote location or not.

Off-gridders, on the contrary side, should be acquainted with the following regulations:

* Local zoning ordinances

Standards for sanitation and water at both the county and state levels

* Federal and state environmental laws, as well local nuisance laws
* Building regulations for your region
* If there are municipal laws which must be followed, they must be obeyed.

There are property covenants which are applicable, they must be abided by.

In other words the only thing you need to do to stay off grid legally is to be aware of and adhere to the laws in your region. However, to make it simpler, I'll outline some of the most important areas in which the rules could affect your off-grid lifestyle.

Chapter 7 "The "Business In Front" Strategy

A typical on-grid house trailer, RV, or home located in front of the property is a typical way to live off grid. To qualify as a house the majority of utility regulations require that you have certain facilities and that most counties require to have your permission.

It is possible to avoid the hassle by either buying an used house for the lowest cost or by doing the minimum requirements to get an RV authorised on your property. If there are any doubts you'll be able to prove that you are legally able to reside in the area and have complied with all laws applicable.

But, being able to access something doesn't necessarily mean you must utilize it. You are more free to create alternative off-grid solutions without worrying about the fact that your operation is recognized as legal. This way, you are able to remain off the grid in a safe and economical manner and not appear to be doing so to anyone outside.

Since a lot of rules are subject to interpretation by officials of the government so doing your best to remain within legal boundaries could be the best choice. While your actions could be legal, it's recommended to be cautious to avoid excessive scrutiny and ensure that your actions appear to be unobtrusive to your neighbors. The most challenging part of taking a break from the grid in a legal manner is the case when people complain to authorities.

Off-Grid Power Is Legal

The first thing you need to be aware of is that in the United States, [self-generating electricity is a constitutional right] [off-grid energy legal opinion. As of writing, I haven't found any court cases which have put this idea to the test.

You'll have to be familiar with specific sections in the International Building Code, International Fire Code and National Electric Code if you're installing solar panels, which are called photovoltaics (PV) systems at your own expense. The majority of this information applies if you're mounting the panels on the roof or securing them to your home in some manner. If you're putting the panels away from your home, as I recommend in my article about shading and solar panels You'll have be aware of NEC690, which regulates installations of solar panels.

Which is the best place for a home off the grid?

The phrase "off off the grid" is becoming more common in the last few times. A lot of people are attracted to the concept due to the technological world that we live in, where it seems like we are unable to travel anywhere or perform anything without having access to several gadgets. Although technology has come far and allowed us to live more relaxed lives, some people are hesitant to rely on it all all the all the time. We think that the present "style of living" isn't suitable for all.

Living off grid refers to a way of living which is unaffected by energy grids. Look at the world around you, whether at home, at school or at work. You'll see that the electric grid is a plethora of amount of systems or gadgets. Think about what you would do when everything were gone. What kind of food would you cook? What would you do to charge your mobile if you were without electricity? Are there hot water outlets?

We've put together the following list of locations around the globe designed to provide an ideal off-grid lifestyle for those who are intrigued by the idea of living away from the grid. If you're satisfied with your technologically advanced, modern lifestyle and would like to know more about this style of living, you'll be surprised to find there are some locations are really amazing. You might even be convinced to take a trip. Find the best places to live in an "off on the road" lifestyle around the globe.

1. Dancing Rabbit Ecovillage

You've probably heard about or have read about Dancing Rabbit Ecovillage if you're looking to live in a completely unconnected environment. The eco-town, which is located in Missouri was the result of a dream of three college students in the 90s. The plan was to expand to a size of between 500 and 1000 residents.

Every member is committed to living a sustainable and self-sustaining life. Although some eco-communities try to remain away from mainstream society, Dancing Rabbit wants to be member of the mainstream. "Although Dancing Rabbit aspires for self-sufficiency and economic independence however, we don't separate us from the rest of America." Instead, education and outreach are essential to achieve our goals."

2. Lord Howe Island, Australia

If you're looking to get away from the city for a few days and want to escape the hustle and bustle, then a paradise island may be the perfect spot for you. A lot of people prefer to travel to an isolated and remote place where they can unwind and be away from the bustle and noise of bustling cities for a brief period. Lord Howe Island in Australia has a long-standing history of conservation-related products. Since the island is home to an estimated population of 350, you'll be in a peaceful environment that's not available in other places.

3. Puerto Rico's Vieques

Another island has been added to the list, and it's not hard to understand the reason. One of the main reasons that living away from the grid is because there are beautiful islands that are inaccessible and give you peace and tranquility that you seek. The life style on the islands is also a bit slower and more relaxing. This time, however we were thinking that we could recommend the Puerto Rican Vieques Island. Vieques is unspoiled stunning, lush, and beautiful in its natural beauty. Its beauty is the fact that you need to do is get there and put down your cell phone and enjoy the beach.

4. Freedom Cove, Canada

Freedom Cove Freedom Cove was brought to life by Catherine and Wayne Adams, two artists. They thought up the idea of a floating universe and worked hard to bring it into reality. Of course, we know that you cannot just walk out and decide you'd like to live in Freedom Cove. Freedom Cove. The reason we have it in the list was to give you some ideas. There are boat excursions to the spot which allows you to visit the site and view the facilities for more of an idea of the lengths they've gone to be truly "off from the main grid." You'll be able an opportunity to "learn about their activities and the way they live off themselves in the isolated place," according to Browning Pass.

5. Tinker's Bubble England

The community off the grid was established in 1994 and takes great pride in creating an eco-friendly society by not using fossil fuels while working on the soil. Tinker's Bubble is possibly one of the most self-sufficient and eco green places in the world since they rely on solar panels as well as a wind turbine to power, produce their own food, and then process their own wood, which is built their homes from. This is the main community where you can learn more about living an eco-friendly life.

6. Tristan Da Cunha, Uk

If you're looking to get away from the crowd when you're on an adventure that's off the beaten path, Tristan da Cunha, well-known by the name "Tristan," might be the perfect spot for you. A lot of people see being off grid to be away from the modern devices, which cause us to have limited attention spans, making it difficult to spend longer than an hour with these devices. Therefore, Tristan is a great option as it's the home of approximately 250 British citizens. Yes, you read it exactly. Tristan is the perfect group of islands that are perfect for recharge, but also to get away from the bustle and noise of the big cities.

7. The state of Oregon has its Three Rivers Recreation Area

This is the first place in the list which is slightly more expensive in terms of living off grid. A lot of people consider that this style of lifestyle demands abandoning one's comfortable zone and moving back in the past. Three Rivers Recreation Area, however proves that you don't need to sacrifice your luxurious life. It's a gated community located in Oregon which offers a "state-of-the-art alternative lifestyle that comes with the advantages of a variety of privacy, an abundance of nature, hiking and a variety of water-based activities as well as other activities," according to Sotheby's ".

8. Polynesia's Easter Island

It's a fascinating part of our discussion. Easter Island is mainly for people who are looking to test to live a sustainable and environmentally mindful lifestyle, without having to commit to making their home physically. This is ideal for someone who is looking to take it easy, and wants to unplug from their devices for a week and recharge. Nothing more.

On this island that is volcanic in Polynesia You'll be able to enjoy many unforgettable moments, and the sunsets are believed to be some of the most beautiful anywhere in the world. The 900 statues constructed on the island in thirteenth century and sixteenth century is a amazing sight to take in. It's all done without a smartphone and just contemplating the beauty.

9. Azores (Portugal)

The Azores are situated in the Atlantic Ocean and are an ideal location to escape from the bustle and noise of large cities, as the islands aren't popular with travelers. The Azores are, just like Easter Island, is ideal for its scenery and will provide you with the needed relaxation. The Portuguese islands are well-known to travelers with experience and you've probably heard of them too. "It's difficult to imagine a more perfect location for nature-lovers and adventure sports enthusiasts or anyone seeking an indicator of sustainability" as per Lonely Planet.

10. Australia's Macquarie Island

The UNESCO World Heritage Site is likely to be more suitable for those who love nature. "The islands abundant biodiversity and plants make it a perfect study spot for biologists and botanists" states Antarctica. The island is designated an Tasmanian Nature Reserve, as are its waterways. In the time of breeding the island is home to the royal penguin colony.

If the natural beauty that makes Macquarie Island unique hasn't convinced you, its human population isn't huge. At any given moment, Macquarie Island has a human population that ranges from 20 to 40 individuals. This means that the island is a great place to get out of the city in peace as you are surrounded by Mother Nature's beauty.

11. Lasqueti Island British Columbia, Canada.

The top ten list begins by introducing another island, but this one that's only an hour's drive from. Lasqueti is a tiny island located off the east coast in Vancouver Island that is ideal for those who love working on the terrain. According to the Lasqueti islanders the island, it provides its guests and residents with a perfect independent lifestyle that some like to compare to the lifestyle of the previous century. "In Lasqueti, people are more likely to speak about solar panels, composting toilets or solar panels than toasters or microwaves, which are a mystery to the majority of its 400 inhabitants." In addition to the off-grid lifestyle, Canada claims that Lasqueti is the most educated town within British Columbia, so you are bound to learn from those around you.

12. Barrow, Alaska

Barrow is an Alaskan town where a number of internet forums have been awash with complaints about the cost of items that are found in every supermarket. We're letting you know this to make you aware of the current situation If you're considering living off grid in the region. One of the advantages which is probably for the reason that so many residents of the region and nearby towns are able to sustain themselves in the area, is that it is possible to live off the land through subsistence fishing and hunting. This should be an enjoyable adventure.

13. Lammas Ecovillage in Wales.

Lammas EcoVillage was awarded one of the top 10 best eco-friendly homes within the UK by The Guardian in 2014. If you're looking to live away from the grid and join an environment that is a community and a sense of community, this could be the best option that you can choose from. It is because at Lammas the entire focus is on people in the group, members working together or reaching out to each other to help them achieve self-sufficiency. "The Lammas ecovillage concept is one of a group of smallholdings that work together to establish and sustain a culture of self-reliance based on land," Lammas explains. We know that leaving your grid could be daunting and, with this arrangement you'll have a community of members to rely on for assistance.

14. Japan's Konohana Family

Konohana Family, like Lammas ecovillage, is built around an ecovillage of people working together to live an off-grid, self-sustainable and sustainable lifestyle you want. The name, in the end was a mistake to give it away. Any company that includes"family" in its name "family" as its title is geared towards the community. Konohana however, on the contrary side, is more than self-sufficiency. the community is extremely spiritual, as it is stated in Numundo. "They sought to create an environment where people were able to be peaceful and in harmony by adhering to universal laws and using one's talents to create a better environment."

15. Utah's False Kiva

The Canyonlands of the United States has been a well-known tourist attraction across North America for people of all age groups. Kiva is special in the sense that it's a human-made stone circle situated within a cavern which can only be reached via walking. While you are hiking to your unique cave, you can disconnect from your mobile and concentrate on the moment.

16. United States, Earthships United States

With a name such as Earthships it's obvious that you're bound to have a blast and exciting, and lucky is us because this place isn't a disappointment. Don't fall for the description given above. Earthships is an incredible amount of fun, however the group and the people who run it take their work seriously. The best part is that they attempt to educate as much that they are able to those living in the area. "We assist people in building self-sufficient houses...we let people discover the importance of sustainability." Earthships Global explains ". It is a place where you can not just promotes sustainability, but also gives you the necessary knowledge and skills to attain it? Earthships is an essential destination for us.

17. Brazil's Fernando De Noronha

There are many of the most popular places to visit, but we are at number four. Brazil is loved by all kinds of people from all kinds of backgrounds, which is not surprising. But, we'd like to highlight that there's more to Brazil than just the colorful and vibrant carnivals and gorgeous beaches we're familiar with. Fernando De Noronha will make you look at the South American country in a entirely new way. The most impressive thing about it is that it has an ecological sanctuary where you can see dolphins, rays turtles and reef sharks, while swimming in crystal clear waters. This is a great place to unplug and admire the beauty of Mother Nature.

18. The New Zealand's Raoul Island

You've made it to the top three on this incredibly long list, which suggests that you're committed to living a life off grid. What alternatives are we left with to live off the grid? What about traveling all up into New Zealand? There's another island located in New Zealand that could be the perfect spot to make the decision to live this way. We've already learned this: New Zealand is stunningly gorgeous and boasts one of the most beautiful mountains on earth and you can be at ease knowing the fact that Raoul Island will provide you with all that and more.

19. South Africa's Khula Dhamma

An extensive list of off-grid lifestyles and places would not be complete without mention of Africa. We specifically refer to Khulu Dhamma located in South Africa at number two on this list. The area is an ecovillage made up of natural houses built to resemble African homes. Natural Homes demonstrates how the inhabitants in Khula Dhamma manage to survive. "With the assistance of volunteers...we were able to set up an energy-powered water source as well as a small space for a garden, beehives as well as an outside compost toilet. ..." While a flight towards South Africa is a long distance away, it seems to be worth it.

1 Torri Superiore, Italy

We've made it number one on this list of most off-the-beaten-path destinations across the world, and believe us when we tell you that that you'll be glad you read it because this is a place which deserves to be highlighted. Torri Superiore has been described as "a tiny jewel in the world of design" and is the perfect combination of a group who work together to create their objectives and the space to recharge after you're there (via solar panels, of course!).

Being off the grid isn't easy, particularly in the present world. But If you're serious about doing this, then you'll happy to discover that you have plenty of choices regarding the best place to live.

Chapter 8: Benefits Of Living Off The Grid Living

In the introduction above it is clear that living off grid is a concept that is not just practical and useful but growing in popularity and could be the norm in the near future in the near future. It is therefore important to know the reason people are choosing to live off grid. The reasons listed below will help you understand the value of living off grid. If you are looking to make the switch and embracing this lifestyle, these factors should provide the motivation needed.

1. Save money

Living off the grid can save you lots of cash by not having to pay charges that are associated with utilities, such as water, power and sewerage, among other things. If you decide to relocate from city areas to more sparsely rural locations, they are in a position to cut down on cost of rent or mortgages. If you decide to go off grid, you'll be able become self-sufficient and thus not have to purchase all the things you need. For instance, it is heating, food, and water for your house. In rural areas, it is easy to find the firewood you need for your living.

2. Independence from Government and Corporate Control

Because of the dependence on the services provided by government and corporations, our modern society living in grids has become subordinate to these rulers. The Corporations and governments sometimes are able to determine charges for utilities and extort citizens in any way they can. The current state of affairs is that corporate and government partnerships have also blurred the lines which used to separate them from corrupting the system which is meant to be serving the public. If you decide to stay off the grid and cater to your personal preferences when it comes down to utilities , you'll get yourself free from the constraints the systems and organizations impose on ordinary citizens.

3. Living according to your Principles

If it's about following the heart of yours and doing whatever consider to be right for your values and beliefs The modern world isn't suitable for those of you. A lot of people have to compromise and bear the burden of the compromises. However, off grid living can provide a meaningful lifestyle that is free from the city as well as the influence that modern society consumerism, consumerism, and all. By depriving governments and corporations of your hard-earned money, you can enjoy the peace of mind knowing that you're not making a contribution to the social problems or corporate greed, which annoys your own. You can live to your own desires, spending time doing what you like.

4. The Trustworthy Infrastructure

In the current grid, each city block is linked to the next block and relies on it to ensure continuity within an infrastructure network. If one of these blocks suffered an infrastructure breakdown or fail and the entire system within the grid could also be affected. It could mean living in a house without water, power or even drainage. Unreliability due to the dependence of other components of the system is unheard of in off grid living. You are the primary factor in the quality and reliability of your system is.

5. Survival

Living off the grid isn't as easy as it seems. People who choose to live off the grid are faced with the huge and demanding task of figuring out how to live a life that is self-sufficient. This means acquiring an array of practical survival techniques and tips to assist you in meeting all your requirements without relying on central resources. Making your own fuel as well as recycling water and engaging in an organic food farming system can set you apart from other people. If you're trying to be an ardent survivalist in the face numerous threats to the way of life today Living off the grid is a good option to look.

6. Reduction of Environmental Pollution

With the increasing number of people in cities has caused huge pollution to the environment. The incessant consumption of modern-day living, with no regard to the finite amount of resources needed to satisfy the needs of cities has increased the environmentally negative impact of living on the grid. Off-grid living depends on the creation and utilization of renewable energy sources, as well as the employing energy-saving strategies to cut down on waste. If you decide to live off grid, you must also lower your carbon footprint by changing to green energy and responsible consumption practices.

7. Insulation due to Civil Unrest in Urban Centers

Another reason for people to choose to live off grid is the advantage of being far from the usual instances of civil unrest that occur in urban areas. It is typical for cities to be the center of protests and many other issues of unrest. Natural disasters can also cause a lot of damage to cities that are crowded, often rendering residents devastated and lacking basic necessities for survival. Living off grid and far from these urban areas keeps you safe from these kinds of situations and gives you the time to plan for these events before they are felt in rural regions.

8. Food Security

Living in cities is expensive and access to certain organic foods can be restricted. Living in an off grid environment is defined by the agriculture practices designed to guarantee food security and autonomy. Reliance on processed food can be reduced since you obtain the food you require from your own garden. Some of the farming methods employed for off grid life include: vertical farming, aquaponics, and permaculture.

Living off grid is just one of the ways you can free yourself from the dependence that people in the modern age are used to. It provides people with the required capabilities and the knowledge needed to be able to live in a world that is full of uncertainty, whether it's the possibility of a collapse in the economy or an infrastructure breakdown, among others. The reasons mentioned above are just one aspect of why people choose to deal in the face of uncertain world.

Chapter 9: Provocative Challenges For Off The Grid

Today, with our dependence on central utilities for our daily existence, more and more people are opting for off-grid living to not just becoming self-sufficient but also bringing a brand new life experience. Off grid living offers numerous benefits, among them having the freedom of not worrying about regular energy bills, as well as the stress of having to rely on them to survive even when they do occasionally fail.

Although there are many advantages of off-grid living, it's essential to remember that living off grid isn't as simple as people imagine. In the modern day setting we depend on central services for heating transport, cooking, and super-stores that are convenient for food. This is isn't commonplace in off-grid living. In order to survive in a rural area that is off the grid, you'll have to be aware of the difficulties that you can expect. You must be well-prepared to stand the best chance of success in living on your own hands. Most of the time, it will not be sufficient to meet the necessities of your day. In this article, we will discuss some of the issues that you'll encounter when you begin to establish an entirely new lifestyle off the grid.

1. Prepare for the common ManualChores

It can be done a comfortable life off grid by producing your own energy without grid power and making use of energy-efficient appliances in the home, many people opt to live off grid to to be self-sufficient and cut down on their expenses. In the beginning, you may discover that you don't possess enough cash to purchase all the costly appliances required to ensure the comforts of modern-day living. This means you'll not have the luxury of hot bathing water that is available on demand or even appliances like refrigerators, laundry and dish washers. That means that you have to be prepared to return to using only your hands to find the water you require as well as wash dishes and laundry by hand, and keeping your wood stoves stocked with wood for fire. It may seem simple, but if you're not prepared, you could be left with a huge mess.

2. Legislation

With increasing numbers of people seeking to live without electricity it is evident that the regulations of government agencies can be a significant obstacle in the way of living off the grid. These agencies have rules regarding the use of water from natural resources, as well as granting permission to dig wells. Additionally, in some areas , living off grid is illegal. This information is essential in deciding on the best place to live off grid. There are additional regulations that control the cultivation of land to grow food. All of these rules are vital in determining whether it's possible to live off grid or not.

3. You will soon get used to living in Isolation

While it is possible to reside in an urban setting but still away from the grid, such as when people decide to live on boats along urban waterways but it is better to reside in rural regions where you can get firewood, an septic tank, and agricultural crops. Rural areas are typically not populous and therefore are very lonely. If you are considering off grid life, make sure you're prepared to live off the grid. Also, you must be willing to establish new connections with other like-minded people living off grid villages and settlements.

4. Remember Winter is coming!

A very difficult seasons for living off grid is winter. In winter, you'll have to be prepared for harsh conditions since you might not have the luxury of electric heating. Wood stoves need to use more wood in order to keep you warm. To do this, you'll need more propane gas tanks, as well as sufficient food supplies. Winter farming is going to be difficult unless you're growing your own vegetables, so ensure that you've taken stock of your supplies to last through this time.

5. Off the Grid Living can be complicated

It is possible to believe that living off the grid is simple and, in many cases, it's not, however, its inner workings are complex. Knowing about renewable energy sources recycling methods, as well as various other intricate concepts can help you to survive. The concept of living a thrifty lifestyle isn't so simple as you think and requires lots of planning in the beginning and precise and committed execution. Therefore, you shouldn't make things too easy, but instead be prepared to follow the guidelines for living a life of.

Although a large number of people are willing to accept living off the grid but it's likely to be a challenge and, in the majority of cases, it isn't for all. A home that is not on the grid will require hands on and anyone who isn't prepared to complete everything by hand will surely have a problem living this way. It is also likely cost a lot when you don't have the time or resources to ensure that your home is operating and require calling repairmen and experts when things go wrong. If you're unable to handle basic tasks like taking firewood out and taking water to the tap and transporting it across long distances, you may need to reconsider your decision to stay off grid.

But despite the difficulties that are associated from living off grid it's not all negative and dark. Off-grid houses will be identical to the homes you are familiar with, but are designed to save the power and heating. It will require a significant adapting to the new climate and consumption habits.

Chapter 10: What Do You Need For Off The Grid Living?

Once you know what off-grid living is about, you'll be able to determine if it's an option worth considering. You'll need to make an entire lifestyle change. It isn't easy, but with the right information, you'll be able to begin preparing slowly for living without the grid. Here we'll look at some of the things you'll need to be able to live off grid.

In assessing the requirements for being off the grid, consider exactly what require to replace what you have lost when you disconnect completely from your grid. Water or sewerage, as well as garbage disposal constitute the primary concern for anyone living without grids, be it in a city or rural location. If, however, you decide to opt for a rural setting, other considerations like the best location also play a role. For those who want to be out of the city the factors to consider may differ too.

1. Alternative Energy Sources

Energy/power is the foundation for our lives. Without it, there could be plenty of chaos in our lives due to. For your house to stay warm cook , and provide lighting, you'll need electricity. There are many options available for producing your own power source to meet all of these requirements. Two of the most popular alternatives and independent sources of power currently are wind power and solar power. A majority of houses which generate their own electricity depend on these two sources of power. Diesel generators can also be a common option for power generation people who live off the grid. This is particularly the case in the case of generating electricity where the other alternatives aren't feasible. Diesel generators aren't just powerful in the sense of energy consumption but they are also very easy to maintain.

2. The Location

Off grid living could be found in a variety of areas based on the individual's needs. For instance, some individuals are able to live on their own, away from the grid, in cities with as much ease and happiness as regular people. However , the majority of people who would like to get off the grid prefer to live in rural areas since there is more choice in the construction of homes or septic systems as well as farming. It is also possible to live in an off grid neighborhood or villages that are populated by people with similar interests. This is a crucial aspect to consider as you'll want to settle in and enjoy an independent lifestyle, without the need of selling your property from one place to spot.

3. Waste Disposal

Keep in mind that there is no garbage collection service for remote rural areas. This means that you'll need to figure out how to handle your waste in a sustainable manner. This applies to the black water you use. A second thing to consider is the fact that laws exist governing the disposal of waste especially in areas with poor infrastructure, as they can have an impact on health. It is taken very seriously. If you're planning on setting up a home on land that is located in rural areas ensure that you are knowledgeable and have the capability to get the septic tank installed in accordance with the guidelines. In the case of the garbage you find that you collect at home, be aware about recycling and ways to transform it into something more useful such as compost.

If you have excess waste that can't be reused or recycled or reused, a dump in the public area can be used. Compost toilets are ideal for those trying to live off grid but don't have enough space for the Septic tank. These toilets are ideal since they can be used inside your home and outside.

4. Collecting Water

Water is essential for living and this is the case regardless of whether you're living in a city or rural environment. Removing yourself from the central water supply means you cannot be waiting around for water to be delivered to your home. You must discover alternatives to tap water sources. This could include bringing the water from ponds and streams and wells, or pumping it through boreholes and wells, or collecting rainwater. No matter what method you choose you'll need to have the proper tools and equipment to complete the task. To get the water of a pond stream or lake, you might require jerry cans as well as the means to transport them to your house. For rainwater collection, you'll need drainage system and tank for collection. These should all be factored in your planning to move off grid. If you don't, you might end up with a need for expensive bottled water. Don't forget that the water you drink is exposed to pollutants and may require tests and treatment prior to consumption.

5. Mail Services and Internet Connection

If you are planning to continue working in the world of business while in rural areas then you must be prepared for keeping in touch. It is possible to use an office mailbox or UPS mail service to receive and send mail in the in the middle of nowhere. If you're working over online, locate an internet hotspot for mobile devices or build the wireless tower of your choice to get super-fast 4G internet in the area you're. If you do not have the money to purchase the required equipment, look for a cafe or library that offers free Wi-Fi. This is ideal because you can enjoy the same connectivity to the internet that you paid for when you were on the grid, for no cost.

6. Mobility

If you reside in a remote area, that is not accessible to public transportation, you'll also need a way for getting items. For certain people, a car can suffice. For those who do not wish to burn fossil fuels, and don't have enough money for electric vehicles, cycling is sufficient. The great thing about cycling is it is not just a means to keep you fit but also allows you to enjoy the beauty of the landscape. It is possible to stop and enjoy a breath of fresh air while enjoying the countryside scenery.

7. Psychological Preparation

One of the most important things to think about when you decide to live off the grid is to have your mind ready for the transition. Living off grid is quite different from the way you're familiar with in contemporary living. This lifestyle requires the appropriate mindset otherwise you'll have a difficult adjustment to this challenging life style. To avoid any real-life shocks after having cut off all connections to the grid, ensure that your brain has been able to absorb the concept. Learn about living off grid and prepare yourself for living without the conveniences of modern life or else you'll need to invest a significant amount of money and time to purchase them for your new life. If you have the right mindset as well as the right attitude, the hiccups and surprises you face will provide an opportunity to learn and will not be obstacles to living away from the grid.

Chapter 11: The Way Minimalism Will Help Your Transition Towards Off The Grid Living

When you embark on your journey to an unplugged lifestyle, you'll face various challenges like the ones mentioned previously in the book. The most important difficulty will be to let the things you're familiar with and making changes to your lifestyle. Changes in lifestyles are generally very difficult to accomplish However, with a little determination and focus on the right goals, you will achieve a mountain and, in this instance, change your life from one of ease and ease to one which is focused and involved. If you want to make a change in your lifestyle to a more off-the-grid lifestyle, you will discover how one of the more beneficial principles to incorporate into your life is minimalism.

What exactly is Minimalism?
In our modern age you'll notice that the emphasis of life has changed from finding satisfaction by what we do in our relationships with friends and family to more

of a materialistic view. Many millions of people across the globe have spent their golden years working for wealth, believing that happiness can be found from the acquisition of costly objects in the dozens. This causes them to live very stressful lives which don't enrich them in any meaningful way.

Living in a minimalist lifestyle means having less, not less. Some people decide to get rid of their possessions that are material and bring along with them the pressure that comes with the effort required to acquire all of this stuff. If you can let go of the many things are not necessary it will allow you to lead a life in which you can concentrate on what you love and, even more importantly, be able to spend time more with people whom you value. A stress-free lifestyle can also mean you'll enjoy more energy and better overall health. A lot of people across the globe have discovered this and are making the change to a healthier lifestyle.

In our instance minimalism can aid you in shedding all the things you don't need for off-grid living. The concept of minimalism is to break any attachments you might feel towards material possessions and concentrate on the things that you're passionate about. In essence, by becoming minimalist, you'll be able to get off the grid , without being greatly affected by the loss of the everyday comforts we've been accustomed to throughout the course of our lives.

In this article, we'll discuss some helpful tips on how to begin your journey to minimalist living and thus prepare yourself to live a life that is free of the grid, that is characterized by self-reliance and more importantly , efficiency.

1. Definition of Minimalism based on your standards

If you're considering living a minimalist lifestyle it is essential to remember that your own definition is different from others' definition. This means that you'll be required to not just decide on this route, but determine it for yourself. To some people, minimalism may require living in a small space with a bed and laptop, while others may prefer living in the larger house but without clutter of things that are not used. If you are living Off-grid living minimal living, this could involve getting rid of all the stuff you have and move to a rural location in which you live in a tiny house with only the things you need. This is particularly important when striving to reduce the carbon footprint of your home as well as being the most energy efficient you can be by using only the minimum of appliances.

2. Find out how you can live this Minimalist Lifestyle

When you have an idea of what a minimalist life will mean to you, it's the time to think about the best way to achieve it. For those who prefer living in a rural area. It is possible to find minimalist living could mean being in rural area in a simple and small log cabin. Other people will prefer to live on a boat that is docked in a city waterway. Whatever the situation, you must to evaluate your current living situation and attempt to evaluate it and link it with your minimalist idea. This also means gaining all the information you can about living in a way that is off the grid to gain an greater understanding of what minimalist living is. This will aid you during the last phases of making the changes.

3. Start working; deal with the Clutter

Once you've mastered the basics about the specifics of what you need for living off the grid You can begin to make changes to prepare for this. This means the sale or giving away items you don't require for living a minimalist life away from the grid. It is necessary take inventory of everything items you have, and assess the value of each item each day, getting rid of things you don't do not need. This is among the most challenging aspects of transitioning to a minimalist style of living since the majority of people hold a strong connection to their home and are likely to have difficulty giving up. To ease the process , it is possible to get rid of everything you don't require for a longer period of time to break down the connection before you decide to throw it away.

4. Just one step at a time

Making the decision to live living a minimalist lifestyle is a big step for nearly everyone. It is possible to ease the transition by slowly introducing yourself and taking it each step by one such as learning ways to be without conveniences of the modern world, cut these items from your life one at one at a time. It is possible to begin with not using standard home appliances for your chores and working the work by hand. Learn to live with no TV , and many more. These simple steps will make you ready for an off-the-grid lifestyle in which the modern amenities aren't available.

5. Recycling is a major component of Minimalism

The concept of minimalism is based on recycling to keep clutter to a the minimum. It is essential to know how to recycle the majority of the things you use frequently to avoid collecting more things you don't have a need to use. Giving items that you don't require a second use for can help eliminate clutter from items that you don't need and also reduce the necessity of purchasing new things that have just one function. Living off the grid also depends on recycling so, making the switch to a minimalist lifestyle means that you will get used to it quicker.

6. Keep track of your Purchases

After making the transition to minimalist living. It is important to track the items you purchase as we tend to accumulate a collection of items that we don't use for an extremely short time. Always be sure to have a rationale to buy something, and ensure that you have a valid reason and that the requirement is present.

If you feel that you're getting off track and falling back into your traditional ways when it comes to off grid living, this could mean being overwhelmed and not enjoying the ease of living in the grid Remind yourself why you're doing this. Every now and then you'll have to be reminded of the steps above and find the courage to keep moving forward even in spite of everything else appears to be saying otherwise.

A minimalistic and off the Grid Living Minimalism and Living in tiny House

If you are planning to move away from the grid, adopting that you live a minimalist life can increase the chances of success. It can assist you get rid of certain comforts you've come to expect from living in a modern way, but will also allow you living in a smaller home. In order to sustain yourself with the least amount of energy to keep almost zero cost for energy, a tiny home is a great option.

One of the biggest advantages of a tiny home is that it is efficiently heated during winter and cold seasons. It is also possible to avoid certain regulations that are prohibitive like building codes with small houses that are built on wheels. Because of these and other factors it is becoming increasingly popular to live off the grid with these minimal constructions.

The majority of tiny homes require their owners to install the toilets with compost, where the compost can be used to make manure after a set period. The toilets do away with the requirement for the construction of a septic tank , which could be costly. The septic tank is also subject to myriad of laws because the waste they store could pose health risks.

In the majority of cases tiny houses typically rely on solar power as the primary alternative source of power. This is because after the panels are erected on the roof/ceiling, they are a part of the home and are therefore able to be moved around the home if required. Portable generators and propane tanks provide a variety of options to ensure that solar power is never out of service.

One of the most attractive aspects of a small house is the attractiveness of a low-cost and living space. They can be constructed for as little as two thousand dollars. It's a pretty sweet deal when you look at the current prices for rent and mortgage payment that you'll be able to avoid by living in this area.

Although they are said to be small however, they are comfy. It is a different thing to every one of us. But, as you'll have the freedom to choose the layout for your small home, you're in the position to develop a relaxing and appropriate design that meets every need. This means that it is possible to enjoy a comfortable life in a small space by selecting a design that is not just suited to your current lifestyle but as well equipped with the right appliances that will allow you to live comfortably.

The benefits of Minimalism

When you choose to live a minimalist lifestyle, you can reap many positive advantages. The greatest thing about these benefits is that they're beneficial to your mental and physical health. There is no need to be shackled to a myriad of items that hold no significance in your life. When you get rid of clutter, you will get your mind off of the sand and then re-establish your life with more purpose and direction. Below we've listed some essential benefits that come with minimalism.

1. Being Less Materialistic

We are constantly continually bombarded with the notion that more is more. We all put in the best effort we can to make huge sums of money so that we can afford more things that we appear to not need. If you adopt an affluent lifestyle, you teach yourself to let go of being dependent on these possessions as well as seek out comfort and contentment, not working to accumulate stuff that you don't need, and instead focusing on what will enrich your life in general. Even the most wealthy people who appear to have everything they want acknowledge the feeling of being empty in their homes, which are filled with all the possessions that are available. It's often surprising how entangled we are with things that are material, but by breaking that attachment, we are in a position to discover an entirely new meaning to what truly is important in our lives.

2. Reclaim Your Freedom

Being a person who is addicted to material possessions you'll find that these items can stifle you and prevent your attention from what is important in your life. Many people are so scared of losing their possessions that they go through sleepless nights thinking about how to acquire more and how to keep it from other people. It can be very stress-inducing and may cause negative health effects. But for those who manage to let go of the need for the material things they own and choose to keep only what they require the sensation of being free is overwhelming. There is nothing more satisfying than a free-spirited feeling of being in a state where you feel at liberty to do whatever you like without having bills or things that weigh your life down.

3. Create space to do what is important

In the case of minimalism the emphasis is on keeping only the things you've always desired. They should be of the best quality, so they can are durable for long time , without the requirement to purchase replacements. This is why minimalism helps to get rid of the piles of stuff aren't needed in order to make space for the things you've always wanted but haven't because of other decisions to think about.

4. Find time to do other things and family

Our modern society is affected by the consumer culture. People spend hours each week on the internet or at the various malls around us. One of the most frustrating aspects of the whole thing is that the majority of the items we buy are soon replaced with another item. It is a time to shop and collecting things we don't really require could be better utilized to focus on what really matters. Activities that were abandoned because of the difficulties of living a consumerist life can be picked back up. Family time could be an important factor in and bring families closer and also. For those who want at improving their overall health through working out, it is also feasible. By focusing on a minimalist approach to your life, shopping hours can be utilized to accomplish all the things that you haven't thought about doing due to time limitations.

5. Happiness

A majority, if not all of the actions we take in our lives aim to achieve some kind of happiness. Consumerism can give a false impression of contentment as demonstrated by the amount of people who appear to have everything they need but remain miserable. It is crucial to remember it is not something that you can purchase that will guarantee you happiness that comes from within. By being focused on things you enjoy instead of chasing more stuff , you will build the foundations for getting the happiness you desire. With more time spent with your hobbies and family, you'll be able to truly content in your life.

6. How to deal with the fear of Failure

If you're driven by the contemporary culture of consumerism and materialism and consumerism, you'll be overcome by fear of failing every time you fail to live up to society's expectations. You will feel tense about this and you'll be a victim of fear and pain. If you can break your attachment to objects you'll have nothing to risk and therefore an lowered fear of failing.

7. Confidence

When you opt for the minimalist way of life is a great way to concentrate more on developing self-reliance abilities. When you get rid of the objects that are believed to provide convenience in contemporary world, you concentrate on completing tasks by yourself and create a sense self-assurance and self-confidence. You can survive with a minimum of resources and thus have the faith that you are able to face any situation effectively. The confidence you have shows not only in your daily life, but also in your professional. The clarity gained by letting go of attachment to things that are material will certainly help you achieve your goals in life.

8. Peace of Mind

Modern life is marked in white noise. Everybody is moving with speed to finish something. It's work-related or purchasing new items it is evident that people are always faced with deadlines to meet. But, by choosing an approach that is minimalist it gives you the ability to simplify your house, but also your entire life. You get rid of anything that you believe isn't helping you achieve your life's goals, and you can focus on the essential things that are important. The reduction in clutter will help you attain tranquility. You'll be more calm and more serene.

In the way that modern society has changed is easy to observe our world spiraling into chaos. The majority of people are focused on things that do not improve their lives, while consumption is promoted as the best way to attain happiness. Poor living habits and work practices that are characterized by stress is the reason for more cases of mental and depression more than any time before. The concept of minimalism is one of the methods that have been proven to cut off the cloak of things that don't really matter and getting the full picture of what is important in your life. This is evident by the benefits listed above.

This innovative lifestyle when paired with off-grid living can boost a person's commitment and drive. By integrating these two you can break away from the destructive practices of grid-based living and set your own route for your life. This system has been filled with flaws, which are evident in the way that people are required to work for a long time to avoid sinking into debt. This should provide enough motivation to those wanting to change their lifestyles but haven't yet done this.

Conclusion

Being more efficient by adjusting your lifestyle to a more off-the-grid one isn't an easy feat. It requires numerous adjustments and sacrifices to become comfortable with and appreciate the particular way of life. The great aspect of off-grid living is that you're offered a range of choices on the way you can build your own off-grid lifestyle. Additionally, the most important thing to success in off grid lifestyle is to conduct the necessary research. Planning and research are the factors you should be doing before you begin living off the grid because it allows you to move from standard lifestyle to one that is completely free.

www.ingramcontent.com/pod-product-compliance
Lightning Source LLC
Chambersburg PA
CBHW071124130526
44590CB00056B/1865